NT
NATIONAL
THEATRE
PLAYS

National Theatre Plays Series

HALF-LIFE

A Play

by

JULIAN MITCHELL

HEINEMANN

in association with the National Theatre
LONDON

Heinemann Educational Books Ltd
22 Bedford Square, London WC1B 3HH

LONDON   EDINBURGH   MELBOURNE   AUCKLAND
HONG KONG   SINGAPORE   KUALA LUMPUR   NEW DELHI
IBADAN   NAIROBI   JOHANNESBURG   KINGSTON
EXETER (NH)   PORT OF SPAIN

ISBN
0 435 23628 8

Set in 10/11 Garamond by
Spectrum Typesetting, London
and printed in Great Britain by
Biddles Ltd, Guildford, Surrey

CAST OF FIRST LONDON PRODUCTION

Half-Life was first presented by the National Theatre Company at the Cottesloe Theatre, London on 17 November 1977. The company was as follows:

Sir Noel Cunliffe	John Gielgud
Jones	Paul Rogers
Francis Mallock	Richard Pearson
Helen Mallock	Avril Elgar
Mike Clayton	Oliver Cotton
Rupert Carter	Hugh Paddick
Barbara Burney	Isabel Dean
Prue Hoggart	Dinah Stabb

The play directed by
Waris Hussein

Designer: Jane Martin

Costumes: Judy Moorcroft; **Lighting:** Stephen Wentworth; **Production Manager:** Jason Barnes; **Stage Manager:** John Rothenberg; **Deputy Stage Manager:** Elizabeth Markham; **Assistant Stage Manager:** Anthony Godel

CHARACTERS

Sir Noel Cunliffe
Jones
Francis Mallock
Helen Mallock
Mike Clayton
Rupert Carter
Barbara Burney
Prue Hoggart

THE SCENE

The scene is a Wiltshire garden.

There is one corner of a brick and chalk-block country-house visible stage left, with a door, leading to the terrace, on which there are chairs and tables and pieces of Greek statuary. From the terrace steps lead down to the lawn, over the stage right part of which spread the branches of an oak tree.

At the back of the stage is a hedge, with a damaged stile.

The action takes place on midsummer eve, 1976.

There can be one interval, or two, as desired.

ACT ONE

MORNING

Sir Noel Cunliffe *is standing stage-centre. He is a bald, heavy man of seventy-five, and he wears an old-fashioned camel-hair dressing gown with braided lapels. He is carrying a cup of coffee, and humming to himself. Occasionally he bursts into song. The song is "Keep the Home Fires Burning" and he only knows the words of the first two lines, though he uses them where and when he thinks fit.*

Jones *appears in the door of the house. He, too, is 75, though his hair remains black. He wears the white coat and dark trousers of a College servant.*

Jones *(reproachful):* Captain!

Noel: All right, all right.

> *He doesn't however move. He goes up and down on his toes, humming.*

Jones: You ought to be up and dressed by now, really you ought.

Noel: But dressed in what? It's rather a special occasion, Jones.

Jones: I've put out your rather special suit.

Noel: The sun's shining.

Jones: Leave off the waistcoat.

Noel: Oh, I couldn't do that. That would be like appearing naked. Though — the sun *is* shining. Shall I appear naked?

Jones: No, captain.

Noel: No. But perhaps later? When everybody's drunk? We could have an orgy. It's years since I went to an orgy. Of course, I'm not as instantly, splendidly attractive as I was then, but — There is a tradition, Jones, a great classical

1

tradition — Silenus and satyrs and maenads — drunken old men with slipping crowns of vine-leaves and huge erections rising from scruffy grey bushes —

Jones: I don't doubt it for a moment, Captain. But we'll have none of that in front of our guests, if you don't mind.

Noel: No. They don't deserve it, do they? What's for lunch?

Jones: You wait and see.

Noel *(sniffing):* It's not — I don't detect cassoulet in the air, do I? You're not giving us cassoulet?

Jones: I'm not giving you anything if you don't get dressed.

Noel: Oh, don't nanny me! Are we having cassoulet or not?

Jones: Are you getting dressed?

Noel: Not until you tell me.

Jones: Then, no, captain. We are *not* having cassoulet.

Noel: Pity. What *are* we having?

Jones: Car, captain. *(He goes in)*

Noel: Bugger! *(he finishes his coffee)*

> **Jones** *re-enters.*

Jones: It's Doctor and Mrs Mallock. You'd better get on in.

Noel: Oh, no. I needn't dress for *them*.

Jones: You'll have to dress sometime.

> *Jones exits.*
>
> **Noel** *puts down the coffe cup, and goes up and down on his toes, humming. He carefully reties the cord of the dressing-gown. Then he practises a smile; once, twice, three times. He shakes his head as though to clear it. The fourth smile is perfect. He has it ready and beaming for* **Francis** *and* **Helen Mallock.** *They are in their fifties.* **Francis** *is slow, stout, pipe-smoking.* **Helen** *is quick, small, sharp.*

Noel: My dears! How lucky you are — you catch me in dishabille.

> *He kisses* **Helen.** *He does not shake* **Francis's** *hand.*

Francis: I'm so sorry — I thought you said twelve-thirty.

Noel: I did, I did. You come most carefully upon your hour, as always, Francis. And I'm delighted to see you. I was wondering how on earth I was going to cope — I've been on duty, you see, since dawn. For this relief much thanks.

Helen: Noel, this really is the most beautiful —

Noel: Yes, yes, yes. Now what I want you to do is —

Helen: But it's ravishing!

Noel: Of course. Haven't you been before?

Francis: No, actually.

Noel: Really? Well, now you *are* here — you see that hole in the hedge?

> *He points to the stile.*

Francis: Yes.

Noel: There's an appalling conspiracy to pretend it's a stile.

Helen: It does *look* rather like a stile.

Noel: It shouldn't. I told Jones to have at it with an axe.

Helen: It looks like a stile that's been had at.

Noel: Good. Now — *your* duty, while I go and get up, is to see that no one — *no one* — comes through that hole. All right?

Francis: Certainly.

Noel: Should a trespasser appear, repel him with violence. The more violence the better.

> *Hands* **Helen** *a lethal billhook. She looks alarmed.*

Any questions?

Helen: I don't think so.

Noel: Francis?

Francis: No, no.

Noel: Good. *(calls)* Jones! Jones will feed and water you. Everything I have is yours. I'll only be ten minutes.

> *He is about to enter the house as* **Jones** *appears with a tray of drinks.*

Ah, there you are. Bring them food, and bring them wine. Bring them pine-logs hither, if they insist.

> *He exits into the house, then at once re-enters.*

Noel: Helen, you're looking very well. I wish I could say the same for Francis. *(He exits).*

> **Francis** *and* **Helen** *watch the door a moment, in case there's another re-entrance. Then they relax.*

Francis: I say, he *is* in form!

Jones: Yes, sir. Gin and it, Mrs Mallock?

Helen: You're in form, too!

Jones: Sir Noel said he thought you might like the Montrachet, sir.

Francis: I'm sure I would.

3

Helen: How is he?

Jones: Oh, quite chirpy, all things considered.

Helen: Not pining for his old haunts?

Jones: He says not. But — well, he's never been much of a one for silence, has he? He always had his study looking over the quad, so he could hear what was going on. And — well, Oxford's quiet enough, but the country, madam —

Francis: His College rooms are always there. We only wish he'd use them.

Jones: Ah, well, sir.

Helen: How about you? Are you pining?

Jones: Not half! It's too damp for me, Wiltshire. I get a touch of arthritis every time I turn around. And there's no life here. None at all. I'm the only servant, properly speaking, in the whole village. There's au pair girls, of course, but they're foreign, and they don't think they are servants, if you know what I mean.

Helen: We most certainly do.

Jones: It's not like it was when I started, Mrs Mallock, I can tell you. A house like this would have had a butler, a footman, a cook, a lady's maid, two or three parlourmaids —

Francis: I say!

Jones: Oh, yes, sir. And Lord knows how many housemaids, not counting the outside —

Francis: This wine! — it's absolutely — *(he looks at the label)* I say!

Jones: Bit of all right, isn't it?

Francis: Grand Cru!

Jones: Well, it's nothing but the best for us from now on, Sir Noel says. He's been through the cellar and sold off all the stuff that's not ready for drinking, and bought nothing but what is.

Helen *looks sharply at* **Francis**.

You wait till lunch. We've found some lovely bin ends. There's Lafite '45 with the veal, and Yquem with the strawbugs.

Francis: I *say*!

Jones: And plenty of both, so no need to stint yourself.

Helen: Fat chance of Dr. Mallock doing *that*, Jones.

4

Jones: There's more treats at dinner, if you're staying. *(He exits)*

Helen: I don't like the sound of that *at all*.

Francis: I do.

Helen: He must think he's dying.

Francis: It's worth dying for Lafite '45.

Helen: For God's sake, be serious!

Francis: I *am* serious.

Helen: You are *not* to get pissed till we've found out why he's asked us.

Francis: Well, I'll try, but this wine —

Helen: You have *got* to defend the college.

Francis: Of course I'll defend it.

Helen *(irritable):* I simply *can't* understand why Oxford didn't provide a bogus research institute for him. The whole place is bogus research institutes.

Francis: Well, his archaeology has always been so speculative, Helen — the influence of Battle-Axe culture on early-middle Beaker pottery or vice-versa — I don't know. It's been more a branch of art-history, if you ask me. No one ever imagined he'd get interested in the scientific side.

Helen: If he goes to Cambridge now, after forty-five years in the college, and leaves all his money to them instead of us —

Francis: He's perfectly entitled to.

Helen: He is not. There's far too much for one man to distribute at his whim. He's promised *us*.

Francis: Only vaguely.

Helen: It's disgraceful to start new research projects at seventy-five. Immoral. And you must tell him so.

Francis: How can I possibly?

Helen: You can tell him he *ought* to be publishing his last three excavations.

Francis: Ah!

Helen: Don't 'ah' at me, I'm not one of your pupils.

Francis: Sorry.

Helen: We have got to have that money, Francis.

Francis: Well, if this place is anything to go by, there should be enough for us *and* Cambridge.

Helen: It ought *all* to come to us.

Francis: He may not accept the Cambridge thing.

5

Helen: By the time you've finished with him, he mustn't even consider —

She suddenly sees a tall, hefty young man clambering through the hole in the hedge. He wears running shorts and singlet, and is sweating heavily. He is an Australian **Mike Clayton**.

Helen: Here! What the bloody hell do you think you're doing? This is private property!

Mike: Yes, indeed. But not yours, I think.

Helen: You go back where you came from!

Mike: What, Kalgoorlie?

Francis: Now look here, you —

Helen *has picked up the billhook and is holding it menacingly.*

Helen: Get out!

Mike: I'd put that thing down if I were you. You might make yourself an involuntary amazon.

Francis: Now look here —

Mike: Oh, come on, come on — I'm Mike Clayton.

He says it smiling, as though his name will clear up any misunderstanding. **Helen** *and* **Francis** *look blank.*

Helen: Who?

Mike: I'm *staying* here. I'm a guest of Sir Noel Cunliffe.

Helen: He said nothing about a guest to us.

Mike: Are you the people from Oxford?

Francis *(cautious):* We might be.

Mike: Noel said you were very possessive. Look, if you want to play guard-dogs, that's fine by me, but I want to go and change for lunch, all right?

Francis *(to* **Helen***):* What do you think?

Helen: What's the name of Sir Noel's butler?

Mike: Jesus Christ! Jones. And I've a birthmark just under my right ball — want to see it?

Helen *lowers the billhook.*

Helen: As a matter of fact, I think I can. Pass, friend.

Mike: Thanks a *lot*. Jesus Christ! *(He exits into house)*

Francis: I hope we've done the right thing.

Helen: I should think so. We've fallen straight for the first of Noel's stupid jokes. He should be delighted.

Francis: I say! Weren't we slow?

Helen: You were. You don't suppose Noel's on monkey-glands, do you?

Francis: Not after a prostate, surely? I mean — *surely?*

Helen: They do say it makes no difference to some people.

Francis: It would to me.

Helen: Not that I'd notice. *(quickly)* Sorry! Sorry! Though you really shouldn't drink so much. Quite incidentally.

Francis *(pouring himself another glass):* Anyway, Noel never went in for that sort of young man, did he? Wasn't it always Greek fishermen, or pin-striped public-school boys in the wine trade?

Helen: What about the favourite pupils?

Francis: I thought we thought he never did anything with them.

Helen: I don't think he ever did anything with anyone.

Francis: Clayton — Mike Clayton —

Helen: I do *hope* Noel's not suddenly discovered post-prostate sex — it would be too awful. It could lead to *anything*. *(low)* Oh, Christ, look who's here.

A distinguished looking man with silver hair comes out of the house. He is in his sixties. He is **Rupert***, the recently ennobled* **Lord Carter***.*

Rupert: Noel not down yet? Disgraceful! Helen — this is a nice surprise.

Helen: Even nicer for us. We didn't know it was going to be one of Noel's grand parties.

Rupert: Straight into the attack, as usual! *(He kisses her on the cheek)*

Helen: We've not been here before. We thought Wiltshire was only for nobs like you.

Rupert: What nonsense! Noel's not like that — you know he's not.

Francis: We know he is. But of course we don't mind.

Helen: Which means we mind fearfully, but never say so,

Rupert: Except you've just done so.

Helen: Well, sometimes one does have to spell things out, rather, doesn't one?

Rupert: How silly you are! Well, you're very lucky to catch this nob here today, because I'm on the wing, as usual, and very nearly had to cry off.

Francis: Rowena with you?

Rupert: Alas, not.

Helen: Oh, I am sorry. Where is she?

Rupert: In bed, actually.

Helen: With anyone we know?

Rupert: With a twisted ankle.

Helen: Oh, I *am* sorry.

Francis: What rotten luck.

Rupert: Isn't it?

Helen: Of course, she loathes Noel, doesn't she?

Rupert: She most certainly does not. What an idea!

Helen: Oh, then it's he loathes her.

Rupert: He's very fond of her!

Helen *(smiling):* Well — It's an old story, Rupert, but it always comes in handy, and I dare say it'll pass.

Rupert: But it's perfectly true!

Helen: Of course.

Rupert: Damn it, it is!

Helen: Yes. I said — of course.

Rupert: Dear God in heaven!

Jones *appears with a Bloody Mary for* **Rupert** *and another gin for* **Helen**.

Jones: Bloody Mary, my lord?

Rupert: In the nick of time!

Jones: Mrs Mallock?

Helen: Thank you. How *do* you time it?

Jones: Ah. Trade secret.

Rupert: There are eyes everywhere at Noel's — always have been.

Jones: You looking after yourself all right, Dr Mallock?

Helen: Need you ask?

Francis: Who else is coming, Jones?

Helen: We know the worst — now give us the good news.

Jones: Only Mrs Burney.

Rupert: Really? Barbara Burney? How very nice.

Helen: Do we know her?

Francis: Don't think so.

Rupert: Of course you do. Used to be Barbara Van Riessen.

Helen: Oh, *her*. I thought she was Barbara Maxwell-Rolvenden now.

Rupert: That was ages ago. She's had two husbands since then.

Jones: She's been called a lot of things in her time, Mrs Mallock. Not all of them British, and not all of them polite. *(Jones exits.)*

Francis: Isn't it *smart* today?

Helen: I wonder who dropped out. But no — we were asked weeks ago.

Rupert: Helen, you are awful.

Helen: I know. I work at it. How on earth does Noel know a woman like that?

Rupert: The way men do know women.

Francis: *Really?*

Rupert: Best he's ever had, he told me.

Helen: It's not true. It can't be.

Rupert: Ask him yourself.

Helen: But he's — I mean — it *can't* be.

Rupert: It's what he told me.

Helen: I can't take that in for the moment. Talk about something else.

Francis: How's your royal commission?

Rupert: Coming along. I ought to be sifting evidence today, really, but —

Helen: But you've stood Noel up so often, and he may be dead soon.

Rupert: What have I done to deserve this?

Francis: She's only teasing.

Rupert: God preserve me from when she means it.

Helen: When I'm teasing I *do* mean it.

Rupert: I suppose you're one of the people who's never going to forgive me for taking a peerage.

Helen: I suppose I very well may be.

Rupert: It is strange how the older one's friends the more they object. It's only for life, you know. It's not as though I were making any great claim on the future. It's only because I was *asked*.

Helen: That's what's unforgiveable. Noel regards it as dreadful disloyalty, you know.

Rupert: Oh, well — *(he doesn't wish to discuss that)*

Helen: Jones says he locked himself up in his study for two days, drafting his letter of congratulation.

Rupert: I'm sure he did nothing of the sort.

Helen: He only came out to pee, and only let Jones in to empty the waste-paper basket.

Rupert: What nonsense!

Francis: What *did* the old boy say in the end?

Rupert: I really don't remember. Congratulations, I suppose.

Francis: Surely he did better than that?

Rupert: I really don't remember. Are you staying?

Helen: I really don't remember.

Rupert: How have you lived with it all these years, Francis? She's so unrelenting.

Francis: Good question.

> *Jones enters from the house with* **Barbara Burney.** *She is, in fact, almost sixty, but she looks about thirty-five.*

Jones: Everyone's out here, madam. Sir Noel will be down shortly. Perrier with a slice of lemon?

Barbara: How you remember! Thank you.

> *Jones gives her her drink and exits. She smiles at the others.*

Hello, Rupert. Hello, I'm Barbara Burney.

Francis *(thrilled):* Yes, indeed! Mallock — Francis Mallock. My wife Helen.

Barbara: How do you do?

Helen: Hello.

Barbara: Where's Rowena?

Rupert: Such bad luck, she's —

Helen: She hasn't actually.

Barbara: What?

Helen: Twisted her ankle.

Rupert: Helen —

Helen: Noel invented Rupert, you see, and she's jealous of that, and he's jealous of her, so she very tactfully stays away.

Rupert: Oh, my God!

Barbara: She has my complete sympathy. Noel hates people being married, don't you find?

Helen: No.

Barbara: Well, perhaps it's being married too much. There've been times I've thought Noel would never speak to me again.

Rupert: I expect we can all say that.

Barbara: Isn't it beautiful here? And marvellous that Noel was able to afford a really splendid place to retire to. Though I never could see why he had to retire, could you? It was only that ungrateful college, after he'd given his whole life to it. I don't see why they had to be so utterly foul to him.

Francis: Well —

Barbara: Mind you, I expect he'd been utterly foul to them for years and years. But then foulness is rather his line, isn't it?

Rupert: It most certainly is!

Barbara: He does so like one to know the truth about oneself. What's *really* foul is he's so often right.

Francis: It wasn't exactly a question of being foul, Mrs Burney.

Barbara: Oh? Are you from Oxford?

Francis: Well — yes.

Barbara: Have I put my foot in it?

Helen: No, no, no.

Francis: Of course not. But there are statutes and so on, you know — we did everything we could — we extended his term of office well beyond the usual limit.

Barbara: But threw him out, nonetheless.

Francis: Not at all, not at all! We —

Barbara: It's rather how Noel described it to me.

Francis: Oh, Lord!

Helen: Don't be silly, Francis. We know perfectly well what he's been saying.

Rupert: He was well over age, Barbara. Some people think it was really rather a scandal to let him stay on as long as he did. The old do have to make way for the young, you know.

Helen: I'm sure Mrs Burney knows that *very* well.

Barbara: But Noel says there was no one worthy to follow him. They chose some second-rate, nondescript sort of man from within the college. If they'd found someone of his calibre — *(stops, suddenly or not so suddenly realising)* You're — you're not —

Francis: Well, yes, actually.

Barbara: Noel is so unreliable. How could I know — after all he's said about you?

Helen: Perhaps by knowing Noel.

Barbara: Oh, I've done that for forty years. *(Francis and* **Helen** *look amazed)* Look, there's no point in apologising, is there? Shall I just go quietly away? I can always ring from a pub and say I've twisted my ankle.

Rupert: Stay, for heaven's sake. It's exactly what they deserve.

Francis: It's perfectly all right. Really.

Helen: We all know how Noel talks.

Francis: He's said pretty much that to my face, actually.

Helen: And we've laughed so often at what he's said about other people behind their backs, we really can't complain.

Barbara: Perhaps you'd better take your revenge at once, then.

Helen: Well — *(long pause)*

Barbara: I feel like Saint Sebastian, waiting for the arrows.

Rupert: You don't look very like him.

Helen: To tell you the truth. I've never heard him mention you. Have you, Francis?

Francis: No, actually.

Barbara: Now that *is* rude! Of Noel, I mean. Are you quite sure? I've been called so many things — Mrs This and Lady That — I was even a Duchess briefly.

Helen: Oh, I think we'd have known who he was talking about. I'm afraid we just can't be grand enough for Noel to drop your name to.

Rupert: Helen! I've heard him mention you *often*, Barbara. I've seen tears come into his eyes at the thought of you.

Barbara: Of laughter, I suppose. What does Noel say about *him*?

Helen: Oh, that he's careerist, disloyal, ruined by his wife — what we all say, really.

Rupert: I do wish you'd leave Rowena out of it, Helen. A man defending his wife's name seems so stuffy these days. I'm sure Francis wouldn't dream of defending you.

Francis: Heavens, no.

Helen: Pig.

> *Someone else is coming over the ruined stile. It is a very attractive, tough girl in her late twenties:* **Prudence Hoggart.** *She wears jeans and a T-shirt.*

12

Francis: Oh, look, another guest. And — I say! Hello! Are you Mrs — ? Oh, God, I've forgotten his name.

Prue: I'm not Mrs anyone. I'm Prue Hoggart.

Rupert: Hello! Noel's not up yet, I'm afraid.

Helen: Well, he's up, but not down.

Francis: I'm Francis Mallock, this is my wife Helen —

Barbara: Barbara Burney.

Rupert: Rupert Carter.

Prue *(sitting at once):* Yes, I've seen you on the box.

Rupert: Oh, Lord!

Prue: You were dreadful.

Rupert: I usually am.

Prue: Awful. Pushing the usual dreary establishment line.

Rupert: You don't remember on what?

Prue: Christ, no. You people always say the same thing about everything.

Helen: An ally! We must get you a drink at once. Where's Jones?

Francis: Are you a neighbour, Miss —

Prue: Sort of.

Francis: I didn't realise Noel had friends in the village.

Prue: He hasn't.

Francis: Well, these large personalities take some getting used to, don't they?

Prue: Oh, we can handle the personality, it's the fascism gets us down.

Helen: Noel? Fascist?

Rupert: He's been a socialist all his life.

Prue: Of course! All the real fascists I've met have been paid up members of the Labour Party. Just as all the really stupid people I've met have been academics.

Barbara: Are you *sure* she's an ally, Mrs Mallock?

Francis: You think Noel's *stupid*?

Prue: Cretinous.

Helen: Oh, Christ, Francis — the stile! We've let her through the stile!

Prue: Your friend thinks he can just stick up a notice and tell people to go round by the hedge, when they've been taking the footpath through here for centures. If that isn't crass,

13

fascist, and feudal, what is?

Francis: Look here, I think you'd better — you know — I mean, I thought you were a guest.

Prue: Possession, Mallock, is nine parts of the law.

Barbara: *Aren't* you a guest?

    Prue *laughs.*

Rupert: Pity.

Prue: Isn't it nice here? So English! Lovely old house, beautiful old trees, pretty old garden — such a pity about the old right of way! Still it *is* very nice. Everyone ought to have houses like this, don't you think? It's such a shame there aren't enough to go around. I think country houses had better be nationalised, don't you? And let out to deserving workers. Meanwhile — *(she settles back as if for a snooze)* Delicious!

Helen *(to* **Francis***):* Get rid of her, for God's sake!

Francis: But how?

Helen: I don't know — you let her in, you get her out.

Francis: But what can I —

Helen: I don't know, but *do* it!

Francis: Look here, Miss —

Prue: Ms.

Francis: Look here, I didn't know you were one of the people giving Noel trouble.

Prue: I'm not. I'm the trouble in person. You don't imagine it's easy to get a radical group going in a Wiltshire village, do you?

Francis: It seems to me you've come here under false pretences, and therefore —

Prue: Rubbish. I came here as myself, and you made me welcome, and I'm staying.

    Francis *is at a loss.* **Helen** *turns furiously from him.*

Barbara: Do you live here all the time, Ms Hoggart?

Prue: No, Ms Burney.

Barbara: Where do you live mostly?

Prue: All over the place. I'm an itinerant worker.

Barbara: How fascinating! A gipsy!

Prue: A barrister. I follow the judges on assize.

Rupert: My God, of course! You're the woman the lefties get, when all else fails!

Prue: When the class bias of the judge.and jury makes the case *almost* hopeless, radicals do sometimes ask for me, yes.

Rupert: The Pontypridd Nine!

Prue: Oh, and the Macclesfield First Eleven. I don't even draw the line at the I.R.A. I even do baby-batterers.

Barbara: Oh, God!

Prue: I like batterers. I understand them. In my view there's not enough violence in society.

Barbara: *(amused):* Do you do a lot of this?

Prue: A lot of what?

Barbara: Gate-crashing.

Prue: I didn't knock down the stile. Your fascist friend did.

Barbara: Do you often join other people's parties uninvited?

Prue: Look, if people choose to hold their parties in the middle of public rights of way, that's their look-out. They can't stop me joining in, though, any more than they can close the fucking footpath.

Barbara: Oh, it was Lover's Lane, was it?

Prue: *Very* funny.

> **Helen** *seizes the billhook.*

Helen: Well, now — fuck off!

Prue: Don't be pathetic. And for your information, it's an offence to carry weapons.

> **Mike** *appears at the door.*

Mike: Go on, Prue. You're not wanted.

> **Prue** *tenses, but stays where she is.*

We get this most Sundays, I'm afraid. *(To* **Prue***)* Go on, off.

Noel *(off):* Hasn't that litigious little whore gone yet?

Mike: She's going.

Prue: She is not.

Noel *(off):* Do get rid of her, Mike. I want to make my entrance.

> **Mike** *comes comes down the steps to where* **Prue** *is sitting.*

Mike: Come on.

Prue: You keep your hands off me, Mike Clayton, or I'll do you for assault and battery.

Mike: Oh, I wouldn't advise that. It'd spoil your whole image, seeking the protection of the courts. You're a *butch* lady.

Prue: Don't you touch me!

Mike *(to the others):* You'd never guess it, but she actually looks very good in a skirt. Great legs.

Prue: Ha, *ha.*

Barbara: Really?

Mike *(advancing on* **Prue** *again):* Terrific.

Prue: I said, don't touch me!

> **Mike** *picks her up and puts her over his shoulder.* **Noel** *appears at the door, wearing a dark suit, with waistcoat. He looks like a judge.* **Prue** *beats vainly at* **Mike's** *back.*

This is Grievous Bodily Harm! And I've got witnesses!

Mike: Where do you want her, Noel?

Noel: Bring her here.

Prue: I'll subpoena the whole fucking lot of you!

> **Mike** *carries her over to him, and turns so* **Noel** *can address her upside down.*

Noel: My dear Barbara, how very, very nice to see you. Ah, Rupert. You came.

Rupert: Yes, indeed. Hello!

Noel: A little local difficulty. Shan't be a moment. *(To* **Prue***)* You doubtless think you're very clever. But you don't know everything. I've been consulting my lawyers.

Prue: QCs all, I suppose.

Noel: Almost without exception. And they tell me, unanimously, that although the public — or 'people', as you like to call them —

Prue: So the public aren't people?

Noel: — though *members* of the public, *with* their members, if they have them, have the right to pass through one corner of my garden, that right is a right of *way*, not a right to stop, stare, chat to my guests or sit in my chairs. By sitting and chatting uninvited, you are in breach of your rights as a member of the public, and I shall, therefore, be bringing an action for trespass. Now go. Put her down, Mike.

> **Mike** *puts her down.*

Prue: But I was invited!

Noel: Balls.

Prue *(pointing to* **Francis***):* He invited me.

Francis: I'm awfully sorry, Noel, I —

16

Mike: Oh, Christ.

Noel: I thought I told you not to let anyone through that hedge.

Francis: *He* came through, and I'm afraid I thought—

Noel: Can't you do anything right? You're no use to anyone — never have been, never will be. I don't know how you dare to show your face!

Rupert: I'm afraid we all thought —

Noel: Never think unless you're asked to, Rupert. It's always a mistake.

Barbara: We were only being polite.

Noel: My dear Barbara, I've already explained to Mike here that you're the rudest woman I know. I've told him you're almost in my class. One of the few people in the world who can stand up to me. He'll be dreadfully disappointed if you've suddenly changed. At your age.

Helen: I'm keeping quiet.

Noel: Except, as usual, to draw attention to yourself. Hoggart, if you don't leave forthwith, I shall obtain an injunction.

  Prue begins to jog on the spot.

Prue: Is it all right if I do this? I am moving, look. Slowly, but definitely moving.

Mike: Shall I drop her in the brook?

Noel: Only if you want to be sued for more than you've got.

Prue: I'm glad all your lawyers have managed to get that much through to you, Cunliffe. *(She pulls a pair of wire-cutters from her pocket, and snaps them at him)* Well, it's been a very jolly morning, but I've work to do, so I'll just cut across the fields now.

Noel: *(pause):* The barbed wire has been removed.

Prue: You mean you're *not* taking it all the way to the House of Lords? Whence the sudden access of common sense?

Noel: You have your little victory. Now — go.

Prue: You don't think I'm going to fall for that again, do you?

Noel: Go and see for yourself, then.

Prue: I mean to. This bastard told me he'd taken the wire down three weeks ago. He'd be stunning in the witness box. He was so sincere, he fooled even *me*.

Barbara: Amazing.

Noel: Will no one rid me of this virulent pest?

Prue: Just going.

Noel: Then for Christ's sake, go! You know the way.

Prue: You're such a sly sod. I tell you, if there's so much as a single strand — *(She clacks the cutters)*

Noel: Good*bye*!

Prue: Cheerio! *(She exits downstage left)*

Mike: And take your phoney populist heroics back to your phoney centrally-heated stereophonic sixteenth century weekend cottage — and stuff them!

Helen: Thatched, I suppose?

Noel: What?

Helen: The cottage is thatched.

Noel: Of course. She got a grant from the county council.

Francis: I say!

Noel: The county council is anxious, you see, to preserve the traditional character of villages such as this one, now none of the traditional inhabitants actually inhabit it.

Barbara: Where have all the workers gone?

Helen: *(sings):* To council-houses, every one. Nor will they e'er return — Nor will they e'er return.

Noel: Correct. But it's far too early in the day for a song, Helen.

Helen: So sorry.

> *Enter* **Jones** *with new drinks for* **Helen** *and* **Rupert**, *and glasses for* **Mike** *and* **Noel**.

Noel: Ah, Jones — good. Now — we've got rid of Litigia, the day can begin.

Helen *(to Jones):* Thank you.

Rupert: Thank you, Jones.

> **Jones** *picks up the wine-bottle and fills* **Francis's** *glass, and pours two new glasses during next dialogue. He gives one glass to* **Mike**, *then has to wait till* **Noel** *notices him with the other.*

Noel: Barbara, my dear! *(Kisses her)* How wonderful! A whole day together, just like when we were young!

Barbara: Hardly that, I'm afraid. I promised my daughter in Savernake I'd have tea with the children.

Noel: You're a *grandmother*?

Barbara: Twice over.

Noel: Good God! And just marrying again yourself!

Barbara: I know!

Noel: What's he like, this new man? Greek, is he?

Barbara: That sort of thing.

Noel: Nice?

Barbara: Perfectly divine.

Noel: That's what you always say.

Barbara: I've chosen this one to last. And he *should* do. He's ten years younger than I am.

Noel: Am I to be allowed to meet him?

Barbara: No. You don't like my husbands.

Noel: Well, they are always such shits. *(Sees* **Jones***)* Oh, no thankyou.

Jones *(puts glass near to* **Noel***):* Another Perrier, madame?

Barbara: No thanks, I'm fine.

Jones: Thought so!

      Jones *exits.*

Noel: Dreadful men she marries. I can't think where she finds them. Well, well — now — we've all met, we've all, I see, got drinks — how on earth are we going to get through the time till lunch?

Rupert: You could start by introducing me to this young man, Noel.

Barbara: Me, too. He seems to know an unfair amount about me already.

Noel: Oh — Mike Clayton, last of my favourite pupils. Barbara Burney. Rupert Carter. Rupert, then a dear boy, much dearer than he is now as Lord Carter, was the *first* of my favourite pupils. The first in time; and the first to disappoint me. Now — no one's to drink too much, I must have quick wits about me, and I hate a fuddled brain, Francis — is that clear?

Francis: Oh, but the Montrachet, Noel —

Noel: Not bad, is it? But you must remember that I'm almost dead. I want to pack as much as possible into my remaining moments of consciousness — and I want them fully conscious, not semi. Almost everything is so boring, I want you all to sparkle non-stop.

Helen: Even me?

Noel: Even you must *try*, Helen. The country is deadly, you know. Absolutely nothing happens at all, except weeks and weeks of weather. That's why I'm really rather grateful to that Hoggart creature, appalling though she is — imagining herself the people's tribune — stuffing the Observer's Book of Birds in her back pocket and thinking she's a country-woman, though she can't tell a buttercup from a celandine —

Francis: I don't think I can, either.

Noel: Well, no one expects *you* to. You're supposed to stay in Oxford, warming your arse in front of *my* fire, while I drag out my days in this wilderness, in a vast house, far too large for me, and far too expensive to keep up, with Jones and Hoggart as my only companions, and — God, I'm getting maudlin already. Where was I?

Mike: You were expressing your gratitude for the existence of Prue.

Barbara: Whom you know of old, I take it?

Mike: That's right.

Helen: Biblically?

Mike: I'm a scientist, Mrs. Mallock

Helen: Oh! (*looks at* Francis, *but he is rolling wine round on his palate*) How clever! But did you —

Mike: Yes.

Noel: Yes, yes, yes, of course he had an affair with her, when he was young and foolish and still too new to these shores to know any better. Not that we ever *do* know better. Once set in the paths of foolishness, we wander them for ever. Which is why I have such high hopes of entertainment from Ms Hoggart. She imagines she's driving me mad with all this nonsense about the footpath, but actually I'm enjoying every moment. It gives me an interest in life — so important when one's been thrown out of office while still in one's prime. I really am extremely grateful to her.

Rupert: She seemed quite fun, I must say. Why not have her to lunch?

Noel: God, you're stupid, Rupert. What *happened* to you? You were so bright at twenty-one.

Rupert: She seems pretty bright. Pretty, anyway. What about a truce, old boy?

Francis: Like in the first world war?

Noel: What?

Francis: When the British played football with the Germans, and all that.

Noel: There was no international football in *my* part of the trenches.

Helen: Do you see all life as war-games, Noel?

Noel: Certainly not. I see it as war.

Barbara: Oh, what nonsense. And what *is* all this about the footpath?

Noel: Ah. Being so metropolitan, you probably didn't observe the terrain as you came through the village.

Helen: I did. There's a church.

Noel: Don't try to suck up to me, Helen, it's much too late.

Helen: But I did!

Noel: Then you saw the brook?

Helen: Brook?

Noel: Oh, for God's sake! Listen — half the village lies over *there* — wrong side of brook for going to church over *there*. Path anciently established via roadbridge up *there*. Hence path only used Sundays by church-goers, few in numbers, modest in attire, ingratiating in manner. Perfectly satisfactory arrangement. Nude sun-bathing more comfy other side of house — better windbreak, greater seclusion, and no danger of shocking pious. Ten years ago, congregation down to two, both of whom attend services by invalid carriage. Diocesan council declares church redundant. Church closed and deconsecrated. Clear to you all, I hope, if church redundant, so also footpath. Desuetude sets in, accompanied by Queen Anne's lace, docks, nettles, brambles, No foot treads path for six years. After *seven* years untrodden footpaths can be closed. I buy house. Almost at once Hoggart buys cottage, and immediately institutes week-ending townee society for Protection of Rural Footpaths, rounds up a few bored adolescents with lame ponies, arms self with 4-inch to mile Ordance Survey maps, and starts opening up derelict footways, trampling crops, knocking down fences and talking about the wickedness of capitalism and private property. Like all lawyers, of course, she's completely two-faced. She only defends the radically criminal when she can spare time from

21

earning a fortune in the most old-fashioned lawyerly way. Fees are *enormous*. And all she actually achieves by flailing her way through the countryside is equally large salaries for her colleagues the quite fabulously reactionary local solicitors.

Barbara: Was it true about her not being able to stand still?

Noel: No idea. Made it up on the spur of the moment.

Francis: Very ingenious.

Noel: Very obvious.

Rupert: Clever of her to think of jogging, though.

Mike: I don't know. She's completely unfit. She wouldn't last five minutes.

Noel: Yes, very unhealthy atmosphere in court, you know. A miasma of jail-fever, and the only exercise getting up and down for the judge.

Barbara (*to* **Mike**): *You* seem fit.

Mike: I am.

Noel: All the new intellectuals keep fit — haven't you noticed?

Barbara: Not till today.

Noel: Oh, yes — mind and muscle. It's all very Victorian, not to say public school.

Rupert: Are you public school?

Mike: Christ, no. Do I sound it?

Rupert: Well, one just can't tell nowadays, can one?

Helen: Oh, I think one can.

Barbara: I should think you need to be fit to be Noel's favourite.

Mike: Not particularly.

Babara: Didn't you find it a strain, Rupert?

Rupert: No, no. Most rewarding.

Noel: Dear God, is that all he can say for an experience that altered his whole life?

Barbara: But it must be such hard work, having one's life altered, surely? And then all the envy! There must be lots of that!

Noel: I should be very distressed if there wasn't.

Barbara: And the gossip. How do you feel about the gossip, Mr Clayton?

Mike: What gossip?

Noel: Yes, Barbara — what gossip?

Barbara: Is there no gossip?

Helen: Ceaseless.

Noel: Really? Oh, good!

Barbara: Does Mr Clayton think it good?

Mike: Mr Clayton doesn't give a damn.

Barbara: Such confidence!

Noel: And such good reason for it, my dear. A *very* clever young man.

Helen *(looking at* **Francis***)*: A scientist, you said?

Mike: That's right.

Helen: Any particular branch of science, or are you so clever you cover the whole field?

Mike: I do physics.

Helen: What fun! *(still trying to get* **Francis** *to pay attention)* And where do you do them? Cambridge?

Mike: That's right.

> **Noel** *is very amused.*

Francis: Ah!

Rupert: But, Noel — you don't know anything about physics.

Noel: I warned you, Mike. He has this passion for stating the obvious.

Rupert: But you don't.

Noel: Again! Besides, you're quite wrong. I *used* to know nothing about physics; now I know *something*. Mike has taught me. Wonderful thing the world — I had no idea. Extraordinary — full of little charges of electricity rushing about — last thing you'd imagine. And then— life!

Helen: Oh, Noel, don't start on life.

Noel: Why ever not?

Helen: Because one of the things we've always loved about you is that you've lived it, not talked about it.

Noel: *Loved?* What an odd word! You mean, you don't want to hear an old man's wisdom, you think you know it all already.

Helen: No. I mean I hate the idea of you giving up, and settling back here, and pontificating. It's not what you're like. It's not who you are.

Noel: Ah. A philosophical contribution. Problem of identity. Who am I, who are you? Questions never off our lips.

Francis: Oh, I think we know a bit about you by now, old boy.

Noel: You know nothing. You know what I've been — you know my career. You know, and doubtless ape, my mannerisms, you repeat my bons mots as your own, you fuss about me, you and Helen, like pigeons round a public statue, shitting on my head when you think I'm not looking. But you don't know me. Not even as much as Rupert.

Rupert: What?

Noel: Pay attention! I haven't long to live. Think how you'll grieve when I'm dead. 'I never heard the last pure distillations of his mind, because I was picking my nose and thinking about my royal commission.' You know me better than Francis and Helen, I said. And so does Barbara.

Barbara: Oh, I doubt that.

Noel: They've only known me as a don— a tiresome head of college. You've known me as myself.

Barbara: Is there a difference?

Noel: Enormous.

Barbara: I do wish you'd told me. I don't think I ever noticed.

Noel: Oh, I do enjoy a worthy opponent! I told you, Mike, Barbara's *special*.

Barbara: What else has he told you?

Mike: This and that.

Barbara: Fascinating!

Noel (*to* **Francis** *and* **Helen**): You didn't even know I knew her, did you?

Francis: What?

Noel: The shock in the air when she told you she'd known me for forty years! I should think they picked it up at Jodrell Bank!

Helen: Well, we'd never thought of you as part of café society, Noel.

Noel: I should hope not.

Barbara: Me, too. My society has always been strictly hard liquor.

Helen: You drink Perrier.

Barbara: That's how I've survived.

Noel: Alcohol, committees, spite and intrigue — you all have your ways of avoiding living.

Francis: What?

Noel: My life has been like that, too.

Rupert: What are you talking about? You've lived the fullest life of anyone I know.

Noel: Have I?

Francis: And been showered with honours for it.

Noel: For nothing.

Rupert: Oh, come, come.

Noel: Literally, as a matter of fact.

Helen: Noel — not self-pity — not now.

Noel: Archaeology, for your information, is sieving manure-heaps to find tiny bits of almost indistinguishable pottery of such crude design and finish that not even Rowena would buy it for the servants. It's rot and filth and rust and corruption. Highly unattractive occupation, really, and I only went in for it because I wanted to know why wonderful things suddenly happened in one place and not another — why art and philosophy here, and not there? And why, once achieved, do they always, almost at once, begin to disappear? Etcetera, etcetera. In 1919, in England, such questions seemed urgent and interesting. One way of life seemed to be over. What would follow? And it so happened that a theory was formed, about that time, about the Bronze Age. The theory was that a small pebble called civilisation was dropped, God knows why, into the Eastern Mediterranean, about three and a half to four thousand years ago. It was dropped at Mycaenae, to be precise. And ripples spread slowly out from Mycaenae in all directions — Roumania, Palestine, Malta — slowly, slowly, civilization, like man himself, crawled ashore. Up the Rhone it went, and down the Rhine, and along the Seine and the Loire — spreading and spreading with gold and bronze, till it came to the channel. And it didn't stop there, like Napoleon and Hitler, it was stronger than them, it entered even benighted and barbarous Britain. And look what it produced! Hardly anyone about in the Bronze Age, you know — but they built tremendous cathedrals — Stonehenge, past the church and over that hill there, Avebury, Silbury — enormous earthworks — tremendous. And there they still are, baffling but solid evidence of an organized, cultured society. And in the graves — such goods of gold and bronze!

Of course, I'm a romantic —

Helen: Noel, really!

Noel: Well, I was. About Greece. About Mycaenae. About that first, proper, Greek civilization. For me, Stonehenge was the farthest flung symbol of a great Greek force which still sustained all that was profound in our own culture. It had all begun in Mycaenae, and spread to here and now, just as British civilization, for what it was worth, had recently spread from here just about everywhere — Africa, Australia, America. No proof, of course. But most of us believed it, more or less. And then one day, at Stonehenge, Atkinson, who's *the* Stonehenge man, was peering into the viewfinder of his camera, preparing to photograph some eighteenth or nineteenth century vandal's name carved on a stone — quite unimportant, but he was making a record, and records do have to be made — when he suddenly saw, in the viewfinder, that there wasn't just a name, there was a dagger. The light just happened to strike the stone at the angle to make it visible. And there wasn't just a dagger, there was an axe. There were, by the time he'd finished looking — by the time we'd all finished looking — axes and daggers all over several of the major stones of Stonehenge. But the carving of carvings was that first one, the dagger on stone 53. It was Mycaenean. It couldn't be anything else. There were the little horns at the base of the point; the only parallel in the world came from the shaft-graves at Mycaenae itself. So there we had it — proof at last — absolute identification — Wessex and Mycaenae were one. It *was* Greek, all Greek! Can you imagine the excitement of finding one's theory proved true? It was August when I went to see for myself. A glance was enough. Atkinson was perfectly right. I walked away from the henge, towards the south-east. There's a little shallow ditch round the place — ceremonial, probably, not defensive. I stood at the edge of the ditch, and I looked over the downs towards Greece. Wave upon wave, ripple on ripple of Greece had come lapping across Europe, and broken here at my feet. And I felt I understood not just a bit of the past, not just a piece of British history, but history itself, the wave upon wave of *life*, which had brought *me there*, to Stonehenge on an

August morning, with the larks singing and — We're only given a moment or two in our lives like that. When we can see everything plain. And I saw it. *(long pause)* Only it was all balls. Stonehenge is far, far older than Mycaenae. There's no connection at all. My whole life's work, book upon book, article on learned article, was based on a false premise.

Francis: I say!

Noel: Yes, well — that's what you would say.

Rupert: But — look here — I mean, is this true?

Mike: Yup.

Barbara: What happened?

Mike: Radio-carbon dating and the California Bristlecone Pine.

Barbara: I think you're going to have to say a *little* more than that, Mike.

Mike: All living things contain radio-carbon. When they die, the radio-carbon starts dying, too, but it takes about 70,000 years actually to disapear. By measuring the rate at which the stuff's decayed, you can tell how long a person or thing's been dead.

Barbara: And *you* discovered *that*?

Mike: I wish I had! I'd be famous!

Noel: No, no, no. He's patiently trying to educate me in the new techniques. He's leading me like a kindly light through the encircling gloom of my own subject. Such interesting things he's told me. This radio-carbon, for instance — they don't measure it in hours and years but— so poetic, science — half-lives.

Rupert: Ah! Very nice!

Helen: But is it accurate?

Mike: It wasn't. Till someone thought of checking it against the rings of the Bristlecone Pine. The California Bristlecone Pine is the oldest living thing in the world. It's pretty useful.

Noel: I always loathed California. And pine-trees.

Mike: Yes, well — too bad.

Noel: I was out by nearly a thousand years. All my assumptions were wrong. Civilization, it seems, does *not* spread out from a great centre — it just suddenly appears. There was no great diffusion of culture, no Wessex glory that was Greece.

Barbara: My God!

Noel: Well, christianity *was* diffused. So was the British Empire. They both misled us. We thought we'd been the new Mycaenae, sending out law and order, and justice, and the Pax Britannica, diffusing culture in all directions. We rated ourselves extremely high. We were dreadfully vain. Pride ruled our will. Cardinal Newman was a shit of hell, but he knew about British sin when he wrote that.

> **Jones** *comes in with new drinks for everyone.*

Francis: But look here — what about all the daggers?

Noel: God knows. Kilroy was here, perhaps. All you can know for certain about graffiti is that they can't be earlier than the wall on which they're written. They could have been done at any time in the last four thousand years. We should have realised that from the beginning. But we didn't want to. We didn't want to spoil our highly satisfactory theory. No one, romantic or rationalist, ever sees anything except what he wants to see.

Mike: That's not true.

Noel: The history of humane learning is the history of highly intelligent but vain and obstinate men fighting tooth and nail to go on believing what they want to believe in the face of all the evidence.

Francis: Ah!

Helen: Francis!

Francis: Sorry.

Noel: Do you want me to repeat that? If you're going to retail it as your own, I would like you to get it right.

Barbara: How can you bear to joke about it?

Noel: Well, I'm only half-joking, of course. Though when I say I'm glad I've been proved a phoney, I'm absolutely serious.

Mike: No one says you're that.

Noel: A fool, then. I'm glad to have been exposed. I rejoice in it. *(takes glass from* **Jones***)* Let's drink to it. Let's drink to the true life after death.

Jones: Now, captain.

Noel: Seventy thousand years of gradual decay!

> *He drinks. Of the others, only* **Mike** *also does so. The rest stop their glasses at various points on the way to their lips.*

Jones *exits, disapprovingly.*

Not thirsty, Barbara?

Barbara: Too morbid.

Noel: After all those husbands, you look for sex in the grave? Or love, is it? And the *life* peer, I suppose, imagines himself advising God, chairman of the Archangel Gabriel's Committee on Strategic Planning. And the master and mistress cling pathetically to *this* life and *my* office. Well, well! Why did *you* drink?

Mike: Why not? There's nothing wrong with half-life. It's real, not metaphysical.

Noel: You deny me poetry in my last hours! Well — quite right, too.

Helen: Oh dear, you *are* getting morbid.

Noel: I'm seventy-five, Helen. As you know very well. You and Francis harped like guardian angels on the subject when you were levering me out of the college. Death is, naturally, often in my thoughts, and I am preparing to die well. I don't want to be maundering and sentimental, I want to be rational and hard. I want facts, I want the truth. Which is why, since you must all be wondering, I've invited such a very ill-assorted party here today. The Bristlecone Pine has scraped off the rubbish and rot which have hidden the truth from me. It's been like having cataracts removed. And what I see, with these fresh but dying eyes, is that I know almost nothing about anything. Especially about myself. And I *want* to know. What could be more natural? I want you to tell me all about me.

Francis: Oh, I say!

Noel: I know what *The Times* will say. I got hold of my obituary the other day. Very boring. Just a list of academic achievements, books, excavations, plus a few external traits of personality. A fool could have written it, and as a matter of fact a fool did.

Rupert: Those things are supposed to be secret.

Noel: A fool, dear boy, a complete fool. Now — what *I* want to know is, what on earth I've been doing on earth? It makes no sense to me whatever, all this stuff about the honorary degrees and masterships and vice-chancellorships and

29

presidences of this royal society and that. Why was I sitting in libraries and on committees, when I could have been fucking or boozing or both? My *unlived* life — that's what I think you know more about than me — the possibilities that never came off, the man *behind* all that reality, the man I now wish to God I'd actually been. From time to time he's cracked his way into the open. And look — isn't this him coming now?

> *They are all looking at him. But he is looking at* **Prue**, *who comes staggering on, covered in blood, and limping. She sways a moment.*

Prue: You bastard!

> *She falls.* **Mike** *runs to her.*

Mike: Christ, Noel — she's hurt!

Noel: I most certainly hope so. The bull's been eating its head off in that field for a fortnight.

Helen: *What?*

Francis: You — you put a bull in the field to —

Noel: Yes, yes, yes. Clowns always want to play Hamlet. They forget it ends with a blood-spattered stage. She'll think twice before she comes in here again — litigious little turd!

> **Jones** *enters.*

Jones: Luncheon is served, sir.

Noel: Good! I'm hungry. Come on, everyone — lunch! Leave that mess — Jones 'll clear it up. It's nothing to the trenches, is it, Jones? Come along! *(He strides off)*

Mike: Prue? Prue? Noel, for Christ's sake — (**Noel** *has gone*) Prue?

CURTAIN

ACT TWO

AFTERNOON

Francis comes out of the house, profoundly satisfied. He yawns and stretches, replete. Then he goes over to a long chair, and plumps the cushions. He's just settling quietly down when **Helen** *darts from the house.*

Helen: You *pig*! You filthy *pig*!

Francis: What?

Helen: I've never seen such a revolting display in my life! Even from you!

Francis: What on earth are you talking about?

Helen: You didn't even *offer* to help! You just went straight in, sat down, and *stuffed*!

Francis: We were asked to *lunch*, Helen, not to go traipsing about the country playing ambulances. If that's how Rupert and Clayton want to spend their lunch, more fool them. Jones is one of the best cooks in Europe, and it's sheer folly not to do him justice.

Helen: Did Mrs Burney 'do him justice'? Did I?

Francis: You seemed to be tucking in all right.

Helen: Only so *you* wouldn't seem so uniquely disgusting!

Francis: Balls.

Helen: It nearly choked me!

Francis: Pity it didn't.

Helen: God, you're so *stupid*! Don't you realise, these are Noel's closest friends. We're going to need them.

Francis: Ah, but they've all offended Jones, and I haven't. Jones is tremendously important. I was thinking — if Noel wants to live like this, then of course he doesn't want those rooms on

31

Staircase Eleven. Why don't we offer him the Old Brewery? It would only mean moving out six students. We could make it very nice for him. And there'd be a sort of flatlet for Jones in the attic.

Helen: Oh, God! All you ever think about is your —

Noel *enters, pursued by a furiously indignant* **Jones.**

Jones: Now, look, captain, you said lunch for six, and lunch for six I provided. How many sat down? Four. How many ate? Two and a half.

Noel: I could hardly know Mrs Burney and Mrs Mallock weren't going to feel hungry, could I? Or that Mike and Lord Carter would prefer to starve in the outpatients waiting room than eat your delicious food at my table.

Jones: I'll have you know Veal Prince Orloff has two sauces.

Noel: I do know, and I rejoice.

Jones: It took me all morning.

Noel: And was worth every moment — every moment.

Helen: It was delicious — really.

Jones: *You* hardly touched it.

Francis: It was out of this world.

Jones: Right. So it was. And what's the point of making something out of this world, if there's no one *in* this world to eat it and notice?

Francis: I noticed all right.

Jones: But there's enough left over to feed a regiment.

Francis *(sad):* I know.

Noel: Well, you will over-order. I've been telling you about it for fifty years.

Jones: Listen, captain. I'm too old to be buggered about. Every time you ask me to put on a show, something happens — every bleeding time.

Noel: It's not my fault if trespassers will go and gore themselves on the local bulls, Jones.

Jones: You upset people for the sake of it. And then — Mrs Burney! Stirring my lovely sauces with her dirty fag-ends. That's not manners, captain. That's ill-bred. Women smoking's bad enough, but at table! Over my food!

Noel: I'll let Mrs Burney know what you feel. I expect it was the blood upset her. Women often *are* squeamish about blood.

They lead such very sheltered lives. They haven't seen what you and I have seen.

Francis: Didn't one of her husbands shoot himself in front of her?

Noel: Yes, but that wouldn't be enough to harden her. I was squeamish myself for the first fifty or sixty corpses. Weren't you, Jones?

Jones: I'm warning you. You upset everyone before lunch again, and you'll get frozen New Zealand chops and tinned peas. I mean it.

Noel: Very well. You have made your protest, and it has been noted. In future I will only upset people *after* lunch. Now go and wash up.

Helen: Can I give you a hand, Jones?

Jones *(sniff):* Thank you, madam. The captain has bought me a machine. *(Jones exits)*

Noel: It's no use trying to butter him up when he's in that mood. Besides, it won't do you any good. He's far too loyal.

Helen: I was only trying to be helpful.

Noel: Nonsense. You knew he'd say no. You just wanted credit for offering. And if he had said yes, you'd only have pumped him for my future plans. Not, with my expectation of life, that I have any. I am dying, you know.

Pause

Francis: Are you — I mean — you're not really?

Noel: We are all dying, Francis, from the moment we're born.

Helen: I think we thought you meant you were rather nearer the actual moment than that.

Noel: Yes, well, I did.

Francis: Oh, Lord! I mean — really?

Noel: What do *you* think?

Francis: I'm dreadfully sorry.

Noel: Are you? Really?

Helen: Of course.

Noel: Don't answer for him. He's a linguist. He should be able to express his sorrow in at least six languages.

Francis: Of course I'm sorry.

Noel: Then kindly be so good as to express your sorrow in a practical manner by yielding me my chair, and vacating me my terrace, while I snooze.

Francis: Oh, I'm awfully sorry, I didn't realise —

Noel: Now then he *did* sound genuine. Thank you. Doctors' orders you know. Why don't you two go for a walk? It's very pretty round here, and you'll only disturb me with your quarelling. Try that way. You can inspect the glorious victor in his field.

Helen: Noel, you are absolutely impossible.

Noel: Yes. Francis, what do you read to send you to sleep?

Francis: Nothing special.

Helen: That's because he's asleep all the time.

Noel: I recommend *Finnegan's Wake*. If you can stay awake long enough to open it, it's absolutely infallible. I've no idea what it's about — never got beyond page one. No one ever has, except Joyce himself, poor old boy, and he went blind trying to understand what he was up to. I did once get as far as page three, actually. It was in the Blitz. Bombs kept waking me up. Can't remember what happens on pages two and three though. Nothing much, I imagine. Goodbye. If I'm dead when it's time for tea — cheerio.

Francis *(uncertain):* Cheerio.

Helen *(low):* Idiot!

> *She hauls him off.*

Noel: Boobies! Here we are. Page one. 'Riverun, past Eve and Adam's, from swerve of shore — *(yawn)* — to bend of bay, brings us by a — *(yawn)* — commodius vicus of recirculation' — *(yawn)* Oh, God! — 'commodious vicus of recirculation back to —'

> **Barbara** *has come out of the house during this.*

Barbara: What on earth is a commodius vicus?

Noel *(jumps):* Oh, Christ, Barbara, *never* do that to an old man! You might have killed me!

Barbara: *You* might have killed that girl.

Noel: *She* would have been no loss. *I* would have been.

Barbara: Yes, well — *(no smile)* I'm afraid I must go. It was lovely seeing you again. And the lunch was perfect.

Noel: Oh, but you can't go. We haven't talked.

Barbara: We've talked quite enough for me. Goodbye.

Noel: Don't be silly. You can't walk out of my life like that.

Barbara: It's how I'd prefer to walk, if you don't mind.

Noel: But I do. Very much. I have so many things to ask you. For instance — I know you didn't *approve*, but didn't you think this morning's little entertainment was nicely timed? Open air theatricals are always such fun. And wasn't it satisfactory the way the villainess got punished? Just like a classic — divine intervention. Well, not exactly divine, but — Surely you got some pleasure from that?

Barbara: No.

Noel: Well, you really shouldn't have stubbed your cork-tips in the veal. You've upset Jones dreadfully.

Barbara: Then will you apologise to him for me? Tell him I was rather upset.

Noel: He knows that. He doesn't regard it as a sufficient excuse. Nor do I. *He* thinks you're very ill-bred. I don't go that far — I did know your parents, after all — but I was surprised, I admit. I'd always thought you very cool under fire.

Barbara: Coolness is not the same as callousness, Noel.

Noel: The odds against her actually getting killed were tens of thousands to one, you know. Bulls don't often attack people, even people as provoking as her.

Barbara: That is absolutely no excuse.

Noel: The most *likely* thing was that she would demonstrate her way through the field without the bull so much as raising its head. She wouldn't even know her danger — she can't tell a bull from a cow, I'm sure. In any case, she wouldn't, on principle. It was sheer good fortune that the bull had the sense to take so violently against her.

Barbara: It was a monstrous thing to do, and you know it.

Noel: I wish he'd raped her while he was at it.

Barbara: I think you're mad.

Noel: Really? Good Lord!

Barbara: I suppose you were always *quite* mad.

Noel: I should think so, yes.

Barbara: But in the old days you disguised it more amusingly.

Noel: Ah, the old days! What was I like, Barbara?

Barbara: Sorry, but I'm not playing morbid games.

Noel: Why ever not?

Barbara: It's sentimental. And undignified. And I've promised my daughter.

Noel: How many husbands has *she* managed so far?

Barbara: One.

Noel: Can't be trying.

Barbara: Bye-bye.

Noel: Oh, please stay. Just a moment. Don't you care that I'll soon be dead?

Barbara: Not after that stupid charade this morning, no. As a matter of fact, I've decided I don't like you, and probably never did.

Noel: You've put up a very good show all these years, then.

Barbara: Yes, well — I'm good at that.

Noel: Is that why everyone wants to marry you? For the show?

Barbara: Probably.

Noel: It's not why *I* wanted to marry you.

Barbara: You didn't want to marry me.

Noel: Oh, come on, you can't pretend you've forgotten. I even proposed. You're the only woman I ever have proposed to, actually.

Barbara: How touching.

Noel: Isn't it?

Barbara: In my experience, proposals are almost always meant to be rejected.

Noel: Really? Well, your experience is wide, of course.

Barbara: Very. And your proposal was no exception.

Noel: May I know why you think I bothered to make it, then?

Barbara: To make yourself feel better.

Noel: So that was it! Funny — I thought I loved you.

Barbara: My dear Noel!

Noel: I did!

Barbara: Oh, I dare say you *thought* it. But you didn't love me. You've never loved anyone.

Noel: How the hell do you know?

Barbara: Oh, I've half a dozen men in my life like you. Men who want people to think they have a profound but mysterious attachment to some famous woman which prevents them getting involved with anyone else. She must be famous. Or infamous. Otherwise people wouldn't gossip, and you wouldn't feel flattered and protected.

Noel: Really!

Barbara: Because the truth is, you're all far too selfish to love anyone except yourselves.

Noel: Thank you!

Barbara: A pleasure. A positive delight.

Noel: If these men are so appalling, why do you put up with them?

Barbara: Oh, we make them work for their mystery. They have to be decorative, or witty, or willing to drop everything to make up the numbers at the last moment. We put them to use.

Noel: Well, it seems a very sensible arrangement. Can't we continue it as before?

Barbara: Not if you're mad.

Noel: Ah!

Barbara: You were never very decorative. And always much too prickly to be asked at the last moment. Your value was only ever your taste and wit. And now they're quite clearly both completely off, the arrangement, such as it was, is off, too.

Noel: Has anyone else taken the trouble to propose to you in one of the great squares of Europe?

Barbara: No, thank God.

Noel: You didn't *like* the Piazza Navona?

Barbara: For a proposal, it's rather public.

Noel: The sun had set.

Barbara: The street lamps were on.

Noel: Casting a romantic, Roman glow over the highly suggestive fountain — symbols of fertility from four continents, and a shameless obelisk — what more could you want?

Barbara: I've never been so embarrassed in my life.

Noel: Well — I was hoping to embarrass you a little.

Barbara: You succeeded.

Noel: I didn't find you very approachable, you see.

Barbara: We weren't exactly of an age.

Noel: Oh, I don't know. You were in your first youth, I admit, but I was only in my third or fourth.

Barbara: I thought you were a hundred.

Noel: I was thirty-six.

Barbara: I was eighteen. I didn't even want to go out with you. It was only that my parents found you so exhausting to travel with, and wanted an evening on their own.

Noel: Well, I knew that, of course. But I thought shock tactics might work. If I fell to my knees in a highly public place, and begged you in a very loud voice to marry me, there was just a chance you might say yes simply to get me on my feet again.

Barbara: No chance whatever.

Noel: No?

Barbara: I didn't like you. I was terrified of you. You were so clever, I hardly understood a word you said.

Noel: Nonsense.

Barbara: And when you were drunk —

Noel: I have never been drunk in my life!

Barbara: Noel, really —

Noel: It's true. I pass out before I get drunk — everyone knows that.

Barbara: My father and mother didn't pass out. They fell over. And you'd just put down a whole bottle of wine, and several brandies. And you went and bought me a balloon, like Daddy trying to make me love him. When you fell on your knees, it was all much too much like home.

Noel: So that's why you walked away!

Barbara: When I looked back to see you with a policeman's hand on your shoulder, Noel — I wasn't in the least surprised.

Noel: But you did come back to help. That was kind.

Barbara: Very, really. Especially as you just glared at me like a gorgon, and ordered the poor surprised policeman to put me in a taxi and look sharp about it.

Noel: I *glared*?

Barbara: I was absolutely mortified. Proposed to one moment, sent home like a naughty girl the next. I tried to make Mummy take me back to England — only I couldn't explain, it was all too humiliating.

Noel: I'm appalled.

Barbara: *I* was the one who was appalled.

Noel: My dear girl, you must have been, you *must* have been. I apologize profoundly. It was unchivalrous, unmannerly, unforgivable. Only — may I offer — not an excuse, but an explanation. You see, I had in my pocket, the names and addresses of Justice and Liberty.

Barbara: Who?

Noel: Justizia e Liberta. Underground organization. University profs, like me. Splendid chaps. Non-communist, of course.

Barbara: What?

Noel: Barbara, the thirties wasn't just drunken mothers and fathers, and lecherous buggers on their knees. There were some other very unpleasant people about, too — called things like — oh, Hitler, and Mussolini. In Italy it was usually Mussolini. There was a very nasty smell about called Fascism.

Barbara: I had heard.

Noel: Well — I played my little part in the great struggle against dictatorship.

   Enter **Rupert.**

Didn't I, Rupert? I was one of the gritty pinkos, who —

   Sees **Prue** *entering, hobbling, on* **Mike's** *arm.*

Good Christ, they've brought back the people's Portia. I thought we'd hospitalized her at least.

Prue: It's only a twisted ankle. I knew there was nothing broken. If your bodyguard here didn't imagine he was a doctor on the strength of the first-aid course he took to become a lifeguard on Bondi Beach —

Mike: There could have been internal injuries.

Noel: Oh, we all have those. From the birth trauma.

Mike: And shock.

Prue: Nothing Cunliffe did could shock *me*. *(she sits)* did you know, you're going to have to sell this place, just to pay the damages? As to the costs — you'd better start arranging the H.P. now!

Noel: You can't sue *me*. I consulted my lawyers. You can only claim against the bull.

Barbara: Oh, Noel!

Prue: I *can* and *shall* get you, Mike, *and* the farmer, for conspiracy.

Noel: Rubbish, rubbish.

Prue: Conspiracy to commit grievous bodily harm, assault, battery — You'll go to prison.

Noel: Why in God's name did you bring this interminable matadora back?

Rupert: She wanted to come.

Noel: Wasn't that the best possible reason for keeping her away?

Rupert: Well, now, Noel, hasn't all this gone much too far? I think, and Mike thinks, it's time you two sat down together and thrashed it all out like intelligent people.

Noel: *Mike* thinks that?

Mike: It was a bloody stupid thing to do, Noel, and you know it.

Barbara: It was much worse than stupid.

Noel: But you want me to 'thrash it out'? 'Like an intelligent person'?

Mike: Why not?

Noel: Round a table, I suppose. I expect Rupert keeps a collapsible round table in the boot of his Rover, ready for just such emergencies.

Prue: Mike, you don't seem to understand. Any thrashing is going to be *of* him and *by* me.

Rupert: It is, of course, always the lot of the peacemaker to bring fire on himself from both sides, but I think, with a little goodwill —

Noel: Appeaser! Of course, you would be. Appeasement's all the fashion now, isn't it? Horn-rimmed professors proclaiming Chamberlain the great statesman of his day. Hitler was really a perfectly reasonable man, you know, and Mussolini *did* make the trains run on time.

Rupert: I do wish you wouldn't always leap to extremes.

Noel: Where else should I leap? If the history of the twentieth century tells us anything at all, it's that extremists always win, until opposed extremely. e.g. Hitler.

Rupert: Noel, for goodness sake —

Noel: Don't goodness sake your rubbishy statesmanship over me, please! *(to* **Barbara***)* You'd never think, would you, that this pathetic peace-keeper once believed so strongly in the impossibility of compromise, he actually joined the Communist party?

Prue: *Did* you?

Rupert: For eleven weeks and three days, nearly forty years ago. And I've long ceased to be ashamed of it.

Prue: Of joining? Or resigning?

Rupert: I'm proud I saw through it all so quickly.

Mike, Is it all right for Lords to have been Commies?

Noel: Oh, yes. Everyone who was anyone joined the CP in the thirties. For a few weeks. It was like being presented. You had to do it to get invited to smart intellectual dinner-parties. Not that they were any more amusing then than now. Awful bores, intellectuals. All want to talk, not listen.

Barbara: Did *you* join?

Noel: Certainly not. I was for Justice and Liberty, I told you. We were non-communist left. Everyone simply loathed us, didn't they, Rupert?

Rupert: Yes.

Noel: We were against totalitarianism in all its forms.

Prue: Clap, *clap*.

Noel: How could you understand? You weren't born, and when you finally were, it was with blinkers. Justizia e Liberta was an organization which operated with great difficulty and at considerable risk against the tyrannous regime of Mussolini.

Prue: And what did Big Daddy do? Write to the *New Statesman*?

Noel: Once or twice. But archaeologists, you know, are often engaged in the pointless decipherment of some much better lost language — bronze age hieroglyphics about the olive crop in Pylos, that sort of thing. And like all academics they're always swanning off to conferences abroad. And everyone thinks they're loony, complete political innocents. Well, whenever I went to a conference on, say, Problems in the Dating of Etruscan Tomb Pottery Figurines, in, as it were, Perugia, I always took with me one or two messages from exiles in twentieth century London, carefully concealed in the uncrackable hieroglyphics of very ancient Greece. So, when I proposed to Barbara in Rome that evening —

Mike: Wait a minute! He proposed to you?

Barbara: Yes, indeed.

Mike: You never told me that!

Noel: Well, now you know. Piazza Navona — June evening —

Mussolini very much in power — Britain not too pop in Italy on account of press, if not alas government, hostility to invasion of Abyssinia — heroic Lion of Judah, and all that stuff, before he became an oppressor of his people, and all *that* stuff — are you with me?

Mike: More or less.

Noel: Well, I'd been given a list of names and addresses at cocktail time, which, in the normal course of events, I would have at once coded. *But* — I was in pursuit of Barbara, stuffed the list without thinking in my pocket, and took her out to dinner, fell to my knees by the Bernini fountain, proposed, was turned down, and hardly had time to rise and acknowledge applause from the diners at the Tre Scalini before an officious carabiniere clapped his swarthy hand on my shoulder. Bad moment.

Mike: I can imagine.

Noel: I doubt if you can. Have you ever been really afraid?

Mike: Not since school.

Noel: Ah!

Mike: Sometimes I was scared shitless.

Noel: Literally?

Mike: Well, no not *literally*, Noel.

Noel: I was. In front of the people, the statues, the diners in the restaurants — I felt like Judas. All his bowels gushed out, you may remember, in the Field of Blood.

Prue: Jesus Christ!

Noel: The shame almost drove out the fear. Control of the anal sphincter — it's the one immutable requirement of civilized, carnivorous life. It's the first, most necessary condition of society. And there I was, at thirty six, a mere babe. Muling and puking are occasionally allowed in adults, but —

Mike: We get the point, thanks.

Noel: Worst moment of my life, but one.

Rupert: My dear Noel!

Noel *(to* **Barbara***)*: When you came back — what did I look like?

Barbara: What?

Noel: My defences were down. What was behind them?

Barbara: I don't understand.

Noel: What did you see?

Barbara: You.

Noel: But not as you'd ever seen me before — surely? I was different — I must have been. (**Barbara** *looks at him in distress*). Come on, come on—there must have been *something*.

Barbara: You just *glared*. Like an angry baby.

Noel: For God's sake, have I exposed myself after all these years for *nothing*?

Barbara: You just glared, and sent me off with the policeman.

Mike: I thought you were too scared to move.

Noel: Oh, alone with the Polizei — yes. Absolutely statuesque. But once she turned back, once I had to do something — sphincter instantly reassumed control, defences sprang to. Had to get away from carabiniere because of Justice and Liberty, from Barbara because of . . .

Mike: Quite.

Noel: Obviously only one solution — dispose of them together. So I did.

Prue: And he actually *went*?

Noel: Of course.

Prue: Good grief.

Noel: My poor child, you're so hopelessly ignorant of real life. If you've ever ordered Englishmen to go over the top to absolutely certain death in a very doubtful cause, and they've obeyed you, ordering fascist policemen to fetch taxis is child's play. It's just a question of the tone of voice.

Barbara: And I thought —

Noel: Yes?

Barbara: I thought either you *were* drunk, or you were so hurt by my refusal, you couldn't face me.

Noel: So you went obediently, too. As I hoped.

Barbara: I thought you'd be pacing the streets all night!

Noel: Well, it did take most of the night to get back to the hotel. But pacing didn't come into it.

Barbara: And then you never mentioned it again! You didn't explain, you didn't apologise — you just went on as though nothing had happened, talking about the Golden House of Nero or something. So I thought you *had* been drunk, and forgotten.

43

Noel: Well, what could I do? It was obvious that my proposal went way beyond your powers of imagination. And I couldn't explain, and I never apologize. All I could do was keep talking.

Barbara: Noel — I *am* sorry.

Noel: I think you should be. If you really saw nothing, you must have been quite abnormally inattentive. You're almost here under false pretences.

Rupert: I wonder if Barbara hasn't actually said something rather profound, Noel.

Noel: How can anything be *rather* profound?

Rupert: She said you looked like a baby. Aren't we all babies when our defences are down? Isn't the man behind the mask always a child?

Noel: No! Balls! I won't have it! Pathetic Freudian determinism! Viennese drivel! We *start* as babies, yes. We have to start somewhere. And we often *end* as babies, if we don't have the luck of a stroke or an overdose to keep us out of the geriatric ward. But we're not babies in between. You're not a baby, you're a lord. Of sorts. Barbara's not a baby, she's a notorious woman. Mike's a lifeguard and physicist. *She's* a professional trouble-maker.

> **Francis** *and* **Helen** *enter from walking.*

Helen's a scheming minx. Francis — well, Francis is a baby.

Francis: I say! What have I done to deserve that?

Noel: All that Freudian bosh tries to pretend an oak-tree is 'really' an acorn. It's not. It's an oak-tree.

Helen: Oh, goody! Is it free-will versus determinism? I always enjoy that.

Rupert: I only meant —

Noel: You meant the usual liberal cant. No one is really responsible for himself. Central European metaphysical psychology! God spare me *that!*

Helen *(to* **Prue***)*: Hello, you're back, then. Have we missed anything good?

Prue: Nothing. He's been on about how he took up arms against the fascist despots. Single-handed he fought the gestapo and saved eight million Jews.

Rupert: Steady on, Prue.

Prue: Oh, but it's such self-regarding shit! There was a war on, and he wants us to give him a medal for carrying messages! He risked his non-combatant status — big deal! *(to Noel)* People were dying in Spain, while you were getting cheap thrills in Rome, you know.

Noel: Yes, I do know.

Prue: Medals aren't awarded for having your heart in the right place at the right time.

Noel: You think I should have gone to Spain?

Prue: Of course.

Noel *(to Mike):* I haven't told you about Harry Somerville, have I?

Mike: No.

Noel: He went to Spain.

Francis *(to Rupert):* Somerville?

Rupert: A friend of mine at Oxford.

Noel: Nonsense — he was one of my young men. He was far and away the most brilliant of all my favourite pupils. More brilliant even than you, dear boy. *(to Mike)* And far better-looking. Black hair, blue eyes — absolute knock-out. And modest with it — so rare, that, when there's brains — unheard of with brains *and* beauty. Everyone loved him — dons, scouts, men, women. As soon as you saw him you felt twice as alive. For Harry, anyone would do anything.

Helen: Were *you* in love with him?

Noel: Certainly not.

Helen: Sure?

Noel: My dear Helen, I've told you — it would go against all my principles. Which isn't to say there's not always a frisson between teacher and pupil, an erotic undertone. Even Francis must have noticed that.

Francis: Oh, I don't think —

Noel: But though I am always *fond* of my young men — I have equally always made it a strict point not to let it go further.

Barbara: Why ever not?

Noel: Bad for the pupil. Gives him ideas above his station. Gets in the way of his *education*. I take education seriously. I've always considered that dons who want to marry their pupils should be castrated, like poor old Abelard.

45

Barbara: Noel!

Noel: I wouldn't say it if I hadn't felt the temptation, Barbara. And with Harry — well, I wasn't in love with him, of course, but I knew I could have been. And when I think of him — There are some extremely gloomy philosophers you may not have heard of, who say the only way we can tell we're actually alive is by feeling pain. When I think about Harry I know I'm not dead. And I do think about him — often. Though he was killed half my life ago, in Spain. *(to* **Prue***)* Fighting against Franco, before you try to be clever. *(***Prue** *is silent)* I killed him, though, not Franco.

Rupert: Nonsense.

Noel: Well, all right — *we* killed him.

Rupert: *Utter* nonsense.

Francis: Too many people died in Spain who had no business there.

Helen: Francis!

Francis: It's true.

Noel: When Harry came up to Oxford, we all spotted him at once. But the first to get hold of him was the Monsignor — God's Mephistopheles, I called him. He told Harry his gifts weren't his, they came from God and belonged to God, and should be dedicated to God's service here on earth. Frightful claptrap, of course, but Harry had been at one of those catholic boarding-schools where they teach guilt along with Latin grammar, and put 'To the greater glory of God' at the bottom of their sums.

Barbara: Oh, God! I went to a school like that!

Helen: I presume you've been struck off the old girls' register by now?

Barbara: Oh, no. Those places never let you go. Once you've been to a convent school, God haunts you for ever, whether you believe in him or not.

Noel: Exactly. Which gave the Monsignor a most unfair advantage. He wanted to make Harry a bishop, a cardinal — some sort of glorified clerk in the bureaucracy of God. But God *doesn't* exist, and civilization does, and it seemed to me a clear case of life against death. So I invoked my rather different idols, and grappled with Mephistopheles for poor

Harry's soul.

Prue: How absolutely grotesque!

Mike: Be quiet.

Prue: Obscene!

Noel: It was, really. It was like the trenches — a few yards gained, a few yards lost — no real advance or victory for either side, just a grim, grinding struggle for no man's land. But no bloody God's land, either, if I could help it. So when Mephisopheles tried the usual clerical trick, I was ready. He tried to make Harry fall in love with Jesus Christ, of course.

Barbara: Of course!

Noel: It often works.

Barbara: Nine times out of ten with convent girls.

Noel: Only about six out of ten with public schoolboys in the thirties. Sport took its toll.

Mike: I don't understand.

Noel: My dear boy, at all good public schools, catholic or protestant, sex and religion are utterly confused. The nearly naked Christ above the chapel altar is the captain of football stepping from the showers in all his physical glory, and donning a slip of towel to go and groan ecstatically on his phallic cross.

Prue: That *does* make sense.

Noel: But if the Monsignor had J.C., *I* had the captain of football. Impossible to believe now, but Rupert was really quite handsome in those days. In a conventional way. He was always conventional — more senior prefect than football captain, really. But he dropped the towel as required, and showed a highly gratifying interest in this up but all too rarely coming young man who was much nicer and more interesting than he was in every way but far too modest to know it. And just those two or three years younger which makes all the difference at that age. It wasn't difficult, as it turned out — it was almost too easy.

Rupert: This is all quite preposterous, by the way. Very amusing, but it bears no resemblance to the truth whatever.

Prue: You mean you didn't have an affair with this man?

Rupert: Oh, we had a brief affair, certainly.

Prue: Oh, good. I didn't know you were gay.

Barbara: Nor did I.

Rupert: I'm not.

Prue: It can't have been much of an affair, then.

Rupert: It was a last late-adolescent fling.

Barbara: Lowland, I take it.

Rupert: Adolescence went on much longer in those days. The habits of boarding-school tended, inevitably, to linger on.

Barbara: Does he mean fagging?

Noel: No, dear — buggery.

Mike: Is there a difference?

Rupert: Of course now, when men are practically doing it in the streets —

Noel: *Are* they? Where?

Rupert: It was quite different in those days. We didn't take it for granted, or flaunt it. At least *we* didn't. We were rather ashamed of ourselves. We looked forward to growing out of it as soon as possible.

Prue: Like you grew out of the party, I suppose.

Rupert: As a matter of fact, I was fortunate enough to grow out of them together.

Noel: But Harry wasn't.

Rupert: He would have done, I'm sure.

Noel: If your appalling Rowena hadn't suddenly dished everything.

Rupert: I have no idea what you even think you're talking about.

Noel: Everything was working exactly as I'd meant. I'd even got you to join the CP so Harry would have an alternative dogma to stay him, while he caught his intellectual breath.

Barbara: That *was* clever, Noel.

Rupert: He spent three months trying to *stop* me joining!

Noel: Of course. You had to be defying someone, or you'd never have done it. It wasn't easy — you're not a natural communist at all, and you don't have the soft heart that falls for hard-line Stalinism, either.

Rupert: Look here, I joined the CP because —

Noel: Because you were young, and riddled with guilt about class and sex and money. You were also furiously jealous that

I was becoming more interested in Harry than you. That's how I was able to manipulate you.

Barbara: Has university life always been like this?

Francis: Not since — Not recently.

Mike: No?

Helen: Not at Oxford.

Rupert: No! I've never heard such wanton nonsense in my life.

Noel: Was it you left the door open or Ryvita?

Rupert: What?

Noel: You knew he was coming, I suppose.

Rupert: I most certainly did not.

Noel: But she did?

Rupert: No!

Noel: I wonder.

Rupert: It was a complete accident.

Noel: Is it ever *quite* an accident?

Mike: That sounds dangerously like pathetic Freudian determinism to me, Noel.

Noel: Clever boy! Then she *did* do it on purpose.

Helen: Sorry, but —

Noel: Left the door unlocked so that Harry would walk in and find his lover bumping and grinding, hip and thigh, with his ladyfriend, now wife. Bad moment. Very bad.

Francis: I say!

Noel: Yes, well — What Harry said I don't know. But he got Rupert expelled from the party which Rupert had got him to join — forthwith. And went to Spain. All my fault. I'd spent too much time in the trenches. Men against men — knew all about *that*. But failed to allow for fifth column of women behind the lines. Grossest of errors. Unforgivable. Mortal.

Barbara: Is that really how you see us?

Prue: Of course it is. We're worse than the enemy — we're the enemy within.

Noel: I don't excuse myself. The very opposite. But — it's such a delicate business, coaxing the talent out of young men. Showing them not only their own possibilities, but the right use of them. And Harry could have been almost anything. He had a tremendous ability to grasp and order *facts*. And a wonderful imagination. And — Oh, we have needed him.

Prue *(pause):* How would you feel if he'd been run over by a car?

Noel: Like the driver.

Rupert: It's all nonsense, this. You weren't half as responsible as you think. Not a quarter.

Noel: I had power, and I abused it. Pride ruled my will. I thought I could beat anyone with one hand tied behind my back. And I did beat Mephistopheles. I was Samson in his glory. Till Delilah left the door unlocked, and — Oh, God, a pun at a time like this! Can Freud be right after all?

Francis: Pun?

Helen: Unlocked. Samson — snip, snip — unlocked.

Francis: Oh!

Noel: Rupert. What did I look like when you told me he was dead?

Rupert: I don't remember.

Noel: You must.

Rupert: I was far too shocked to notice.

Noel: Come on, come on! I must have looked stunned, at least. I said something? I showed some ordinary human emotion?

Rupert: If you want people to study your face at moments of crisis, Noel, you really mustn't sit with the light behind you.

Noel: So — neither you nor Barbara saw what I really looked like at two of the greatest crises of my life. Perhaps my face never did give me away. Perhaps there was nothing to give. Odd. I felt there was.

Helen: Excuse me. Sorry, but —

Noel: Oh, shut up Helen, for God's sake!

Barbara: Was all this just before or just after you proposed to me?

Noel: Before, before. Why do you think I proposed at all?

Barbara: You *said,* because you loved me.

Noel: I said, I said! Harry's death was a stone on my heart.

Barbara: I think it *was* him you loved, Noel.

Noel: No, no, no! It was out of the question — I never fell in love with him, or any of them, ever.

Barbara: He sounds a much more likely reason for never marrying than me.

Noel: I wanted to change my life. I couldn't bear myself. I couldn't make sense of anything. Harry was dead in Spain, and I was carrying messages to Rome — but why? Why anything? Of course I've never known, really. Except in scholarship. That seemed a form of certainty, retrieving those bits and pieces from the past, while the present — Does everyone live like me from hour to hour and day to day, clutching at moments, trying to stop the terrible munching away of time? Failing, of course, but hoping, just once in a year or two years, or five or ten, hoping to hold the whole thing clear in my head, to make sense of it — some kind of sense, however brief, before the munching starts again, and everything's back to that remorseless chewing and digestion? All my life I've tried to be a rational man. I'm not one, of course. I'm as silly and irrational as everyone else. My bowels betray me. If I knew who me was, I might begin to understand, but — *(pause)*

Helen: You're rambling, Noel. No rambling.

Noel: I am *not* rambling. I'm telling you why I asked Barbara to marry me.

Barbara: Oh!

Noel: I'd killed him. The future I'd built with such pride in myself and my powers was — in a grave in Spain. You say I looked like a baby. I felt like one. The whole experience of life was utterly baffling. And I looked at my life, and saw there was one thing obviously wrong with it. I thought you might save me from a life without love.

Prue: Christ, if there's one thing I hate more than a male chauvinist pig, it's a male chauvinist pussycat.

Noel: Quite right. A sloppy, self-pitying, self-hating, middle-aged man, and a beautiful young girl — ordinary, human, disgusting. It would have been like sacrificing a virgin.

Barbara: Literally, as it happens.

Noel: Well, in those days, we rather took that for granted in young girls.

Barbara: And so you planned that whole thing — those outdoor theatricals in the Piazza Navona?

Noel: Of course not.

Barbara: You said you did.

51

Noel: I always have excellent reasons afterwards for why I've done something, haven't you? Before I've done it, I'm like everyone else — entirely in the dark.

Barbara: So it *was* the drink!

Noel: Partly. Mainly, though, the misery, the desire for salvation. And you, of course. You were amazingly beautiful. Together, you and the drink and the self-pity quite overcame me. Though to tell you the absolute truth, as I fell to my knees, I was so surprised I thought I must be having a stroke. Since then I've thought perhaps that was the real me, down on those knees. But perhaps not. Perhaps not.

Barbara *(pause):* I've never been in love, either. Perhaps we would have got on.

Noel: My dear —

Barbara: I've often been happy. I like sex. I like men. But I've never been in love.

Helen: No?

Barbara: With that in common —

Noel: But you have been loved.

Barbara: Oh, that. That's very overrated.

Noel: Is it? Oh, good.

Helen: Of course you've been loved, Noel. We all love you.
   Silence.

Barbara: I was in bed once with my second husband. Such a nice man. He was the one who died. And we were making love in an ordinary, pleasant way, when he suddenly seized me. Really gripped me and held me, so it almost hurt. And he said 'You've got to love me.' He looked quite mad, our faces were so close. 'You've got to,' he said. It made me cry. I felt so sorry for him. Grateful in a way. But sorry, mainly.

Prue: You people! You've got no more idea of love than politics!

Noel: Do you think you do any better?

Prue: I bloody hope so.

Noel: Rupert's done better. Haven't you, Rupert?

Rupert: Well, it always strikes us as very odd, but we do seem to be unusual. We love each other more the more we're together.

Noel: It's true. Their bliss is so domestic it makes you sick.

Rupert: I'm afraid it's you who seem sick, Noel. All this brooding on the past — it's not very healthy, really is it?

Noel: You don't understand anything. I've been buried all my life. I'm trying to scrape my way up to light and air.

Jones enters.

Jones: Do you want tea out here, captain, or in?

Barbara: Oh, good Lord, tea! I must fly!

Noel: Oh, do stay. You're too late now. Please stay.

Barbara: I can't. I promised the children.

Noel: Bugger the children. Let them get used to broken promises. Let them taste reality as soon as possible.

Barbara: I'll just be in time.

Noel: I suppose you think of them as your future.

Barbara: In a way.

Noel: How nice. My only future is as bones. In my will — *(he pauses and looks at* Helen *and* Francis*)* — I've laid it down that I am to be buried, not cremated. An archaeologist should leave remains. But I want one of those tubes coming out of the coffin in case I'm still alive.

Jones: Are you having tea out here or not, captain?

Noel: I'm having it in. Tired of out here. The open air brings on too much emotion.

Jones: Thought so. Tea's served in the drawing-room, then, sir.

Noel: Thank you.

Jones exits.

Francis: Jolly good! Amazing how a good lunch makes you ravenous for tea.

Mike: Christ, I just remembered. I didn't *have* any lunch!

Noel: In you go, then. Go on, Helen.

Prue: I'm not moving, you realise that.

Noel: Not hungry?

Prue: Very hungry. But I've not been asked.

Noel: It's never stopped you making free with my property before, why let it now?

Prue: Entering is a much more serious crime than trespass.

Noel: Oh, come on!

Prue: All right. But someone will have to help me. *(*Mike *and* Rupert *go to her)* Thanks.

Noel: Good God, she knows the word.

53

Mike, Prue, Rupert, Helen *and* **Francis** *go in.*

Barbara: Goodbye, Noel.

Noel: Goodbye. *(kisses her)* You will come again, won't you?

Barbara: Of course.

Noel: And you do see — I may have been only a bore to you, but you've been very much more to me.

Barbara: Oh, you've been a great many things, Noel, too many of them exasperating, but you've never been a bore.

Noel: Oh, but that ghastly night in Rome! I mean — the horror of it!

Barbara: Well, now — since you've been so honest this afternoon — You *have* been honest, haven't you?

Noel: I've tried to be.

Barbara: Then — the reason I looked back, the reason I *came* back, after I'd walked away — Well, actually, I'd decided to say yes.

Noel: You — *what?*

Barbara: Oh, don't get me wrong. I hadn't suddenly fallen in love with you or anything. I'd simply decided that life with you would be infinitely better than life with Mummy and Daddy.

Noel: Barbara!

Barbara: They were awful, you know. I mean, *awful.* But then you bundled me off and — Well —

Noel: Oh, my God! My *God,* Barbara! You mean we *might* have married, we might have —

Barbara: No, no. Of course not. Nothing would ever have come of it. It was only desperation on my part. Just as it seems to have been desperation on yours.

Noel: Mutual desperation can be a very good basis for marriage.

Barbara: Believe me — no. And anyway, think how appalled you'd have been next morning!

Noel: Nonsense! I should have been exalted!

Barbara: It wouldn't have lasted your first cup of coffee. No, nothing could possibly have come of it. But you gave me the idea, Noel, and I've always been grateful.

Noel: What idea?

Barbara: That I could get away. That I was — not unattractive. That someone might conceivably want me enough to marry me.

54

Noel: Oh, but you knew that already.

Barbara: Actually not. I *was* straight out of the convent, you know.

Noel: You'd have found out soon enough.

Barbara: Oh, I dare say. But you were the actual first to let me know.

Noel: Good God. And is *that* why you've put up with me all these years?

Barbara: People who aren't too good at love, do often make up for it by being sentimental, you know.

Noel: Oh, God, why *didn't* we marry? We'd have been such a splendid pair! It might have been wonderful! It might have made all the difference! To both of us.

Barbara: No. It's a lovely thought. But — no.

Noel: No. But all the same —

Barbara: Goodbye, my dear.

Noel: Goodbye. And thankyou — thankyou.

> **Rupert** *comes out of the house.*

Rupert: Are you off, then, Barbara?

Barbara: I am. Goodbye, Noel. Goodbye, Rupert.

Rupert: Goodbye.

> **Barbara** *goes.* **Rupert** *comes to join* **Noel.**

Noel: Ah, what a woman, what a woman!

Rupert: Oh, splendid. Pity about the husbands.

Noel: Yes, shits of hell, all of them. Even the one who died. Beautiful women always have dreadful taste in men.

Rupert: Yes.

Noel: Well come on — tea.

Rupert: No, I must go too, I'm afraid.

Noel: Nonsense.

Rupert: I promised Rowena —

Noel: Oh, well then — goodbye!

Rupert: Look here — I do wish you *wouldn't* brood on the past so much, old boy.

Noel: Why not? What else should I brood on in my last years?

Rupert: You're getting a bit — well, morbid, you know. And — well — things really weren't quite how you imagine. Harry and I did have minds of our own.

Noel: Indeed you did. Bodies too.

Rupert: You weren't actually God. I mean, we weren't plasticene.

Noel: *You* were. In the hands of Rowena.

Rupert: We did laugh about you sometimes.

Noel: So I should hope.

Rupert: I mean —

Noel: You mean, you can't bear the idea that you weren't a fully independent personality, my peer for life in every way, when in fact if it hadn't been for me you'd've been no one at all. Well, you must bear it, and be grateful.

Rupert: Rowena says —

Noel: And don't mention that interfering little bitch's name to me again. I'd quite forgotten *how* much I detest her.

Rupert: I've never quarrelled with you, Noel, and I'm not going to now, but —

Noel: You *are* going to now.

Rupert: I don't mind what you say about me and Harry. But I do mind, very much, the way you talk about Rowena in front of other people. I'm used to you, of course, and I accept it as part of your deliberate bad taste, and so on. But other people don't know you as well as I do, and it's not, actually, very pleasant for me to hear you calling her names in front of them.

Noel: You think it's just a matter of *taste*?

Rupert: Francis and Helen, for instance —

Noel: Oh, I see, I see! They've been repeating me, as usual. To your face! *Aren't* they tactless?

Rupert: I don't mind playing buffoon to you —

Noel: My dear boy, as a buffoon, you'd never even get a job at Butlins.

Rupert: Well, your butt, then. To remain your friend for very long one has, frankly, to have a pretty thick skin. But Rowena's a sensitive woman —

Noel: *Rowena? Sensitive?*

Rupert: You might consider just how insensitive it is of you.

Noel: Oh, but I'm impossible. Everyone knows that.

Rupert: Sometimes you go much too far.

Noel: Thank you. I will, of course, reconsider my conduct in the light of what you have to say. Perhaps you have further advice?

Rupert: Yes, actually. That business this morning —

Noel: Didn't quite come off, did it? I meant to kill her.

Rupert: If you're not careful, you'll get yourself locked up.

Noel: But prisons are so comfortable these days.

Rupert: In a loony bin.

Noel: Oh, *you* think I'm mad, too! I *see*! I thought you thought I was immoral, or joking, or ill-advised.

Rupert: I didn't say that.

Noel: You are the most poisonous little creep, Rupert. You're so clever and able and distinguished and pathetically second-rate. A life peer! Couldn't even get a proper title!

Rupert: They don't give them, nowadays. And you're only jealous. I haven't forgotten your letter of congratulations.

Noel: Of course I'm jealous! I made you, and what do I get? A miserable, common or garden knighthood!

Rupert: You really must get out of this idea that you 'made' anyone. You helped me a great deal when I was young, and I will always be grateful. But I am not your offspring, in any sense whatever. And you're quite wrong about Harry, Noel. You always were. You never understood him at all.

Noel: *I* never understood him!

Rupert: If ever there was a case of love being blind —

Noel: I did not love Harry Somerville!

Rupert *(smiling):* No, no, of course not!

Noel: I did *not*!

Rupert: My dear Noel, the more you protest that more obvious it is to everyone that you did.

Noel: Oh — fuck off!

Rupert: If you really insist on digging up the past, do remember that you've spent most of your life behind the medieval walls of an Oxford college. Oxford's well known to protect people from reality. A great preserver of self-delusions.

Noel: I have no delusions about Harry.

Rupert: I don't know why you won't face it. You say you want to know the truth, but you refuse to see it when it's staring you in the face.

Noel: What do you know about the truth!

Rupert: I know you. And I also knew Harry very much better than you did.

Noel: You know nothing!

Rupert: I went to bed with him, which I take it from your protestations of principle you didn't.

Noel: Of course not!

Rupert: You wouldn't feel at all the same about him if you had. Harry wasn't one of us moderate, rational men. He was an extremist in everything.

Noel: Well?

Rupert: He wasn't humble. He was a raging masochist. He wanted me to do things — I can tell you, Rowena saved me in the nick of time.

Noel: And destroyed *him*!

Rupert: He wanted to be destroyed. He loved it that you and the Monsignor were tearing him apart. You know the old Spanish punishment for traitors? Two trees bent together, one leg tied to each? He wanted *that*. He told me about it. He choked with excitement at the thought — he literally slavered.

Noel *(pause)*: How *dare* you? Harry, my Harry —

Rupert: As a matter of fact, something like that is what he actually got.

Noel: What?

Rupert: He did some openly, deliberately treacherous thing — signalled to the enemy, I think. They had a drumhead court martial, and — Well, it's impossible to establish what did happen, but it was something very nasty.

Pause.

Noel: Go away.

Rupert: I'm sorry. I think those things are better not said, myself. But you really forced me to tell you.

Noel: Go away! Go away, go away!

Rupert: Sorry, Noel. I won't disturb the others. Say goodbye to them for me, won't you? See you soon.

> **Rupert** *touches him gently on the shoulder.* **Noel** *makes no response. He seems shattered and stunned.* **Rupert** *goes.*
> *After a moment,* **Noel** *gives a great moaning wail.*
> **Jones** *appears in the door.*

Jones: Captain! You told me Lord Carter was staying for dinner, and now he's just said goodbye to me! I won't have it! I warned you!

He sees that **Noel** *is desolate, and goes quickly to him.*
Here, here, what's this? Whatever's the matter? Come on now, Captain, this won't do, will it? Come on now.

He takes **Noel's** *arm and begins to lead him in.*

CURTAIN

ACT THREE

EVENING

Though the stage gets gradually darker through the act, it never gets more than late summer evening.

The stage is empty. Then **Mike** *comes out of the house and on to the terrace. He seems apprehensive. After a moment* **Prue** *appears in the door.*

Prue: Alone at last!

      Mike *moves quickly from the terrace downstage right.*

Prue: Oh, come on, Mike.

Mike: Look, you can see he's very upset. Why not do the decent thing for once and go home?

Prue: But he asked me to stay.

Mike: That was before.

Prue: Anyway, I can't go home unless you take me. *(she hops to a chair and sits)* You're going to have to talk to me sometime, you know.

Mike: I don't see any point. It won't get us anywhere.

Prue: Us! We're on the right track, anyway.

Mike: I don't have anything to say, Prue.

Prue: I do.

Mike: Oh, I'm sure. *(Pause, then resigned)* Well — go ahead.

Prue: Actually, I don't know where to begin.

Mike: How have you been?

Prue: Not too good.

Mike: I'm sorry.

Prue: Are you?

Mike: Yes. Though I have to say I think it's your own doing.

60

Prue: Could be. Could well be. How have *you* been?

Mike: Fine. Fine.

Prue: Sure?

Mike: Absolutely.

Prue: Good. I'm glad. Really I am.

Mike *(pause):* I'm very sorry about what happened this morning.

Prue: Thank you.

Mike: But you know, you did have it coming to you.

Prue: Oh. Does that mean you helped set it up?

Mike: Christ, no. You should know me better than that.

Prue: I *thought* I did.

Mike: Look — don't you think it's time to drop all this? You're not getting anywhere. You're not even annoying Noel — he's revelling in it.

Prue: So it seems.

Mike: And though I'm *not* enjoying it, it's not getting you anywhere with me, either, I can tell you.

Prue: Seems not.

Mike: Then — why not?

Prue: Because I can't bear the thought of that old monster corrupting poor little innocent *you*.

Mike: Don't be silly.

Prue: I don't mean *physically*. I wouldn't mind that. Anyway, I believe him — he wouldn't touch you. I shouldn't think he's touched anyone in years. But one small whiff of upper-class English culture — and look at you. I bet you never even crossed your legs.

Mike: As far as I'm concerned, six months with Noel has done more for me than Sydney and Cambridge put together.

Prue: You're just round-heeled for the old country, like all colonials.

Mike: Go ahead. Patronize me. Just remember you grew up here, you had all these things you despise a long time before you decided to despise them.

Prue: Sorry. That was cheap, I admit. But —

Mike: It's about time you learned that it's not the end of swimming for the whole human race just because *you* don't like the water.

61

Prue: It's not the water itself. It's the baptism that goes with it. Liberal humanists believe in total immersion, Mike. He'll shove you right under. I'm not sure you're not half-drowned already.

Mike: You can't think much of me, then. And you've forgotten I was a lifeguard.

Prue: *You've* forgotten what they put on the lifeguard's gravestone. 'He saved others; himself he could not save.'

Mike: So you actually know the bible.

Prue: Oh, it comes in useful in court. With the older judges.

Mike: I bet! But if only you could stop haranguing the jury for five minutes, Prue, and listen to him —

Prue: I've been listening all afternoon!

Mike: Well, then — he's not what you imagined, is he?

Prue: He's *exactly* what I imagined! Clever, cultivated, witty, moderately liberal, probably honourable, emotionally impoverished and absolutely armour-plated!

Mike: You can hardly say that now.

Prue: He's tougher than I am, anyway. He certainly seems to have no problem keeping you away from me.

Mike: It's not like that.

Prue: It's how it seems to me.

Mike: You broke it up, Prue, not me. If you're sorry you did — that has nothing whatever to do with Noel.

Prue: Of course it does. When he was talking about that man in the Spanish civil war, I thought — but he's talking about Mike! About me and Mike! He's fighting with me now for Mike's soul!

Mike: Look, will you kindly get it out of your head that I am somehow up for grabs!

Prue: Sorry — sorry —

Mike: I am perfectly capable of looking after my own soul, without any help from you, Noel, or anyone else! And I'm pretty damned sick of the way you talk about me as though I was Sillyputty. I'm not going to be pulled every which way by *any one,* and I wish to Christ you'd *get* that!

Prue: But I don't think you realise the *danger* you're in. I mean, six months ago, you were almost a radical.

Mike: And haven't I grown up?

Prue: No. I'd say you'd been seduced.

Mike: Yes, well, I'm not interested any more in what you think. One of the things I've learned recently is that people who rant on about freedom only want it for themselves, in order to tell everyone else what to do. And I'm sorry, I'm not going to be told.

Prue: That's cheap, Mike.

Mike: Too bad. It happens also to be true. And I didn't want this conversation in the first place.

> *Moving towards stile.*

Prue: Where are you going?

Mike: For a walk.

Prue: Mike! You can't just walk out — not now! Mike, we're in the middle of a conversation!

> **Mike** *climbs stile and goes.*

Mike! *(stands)* Mike, come back here! *Mike! (pause)* Oh, *shit.*

> **Noel** *appears from the house in his dressing-gown. He is in deep depression.*

Noel: Is something the matter?

Prue: No. No — nothing.

Noel: Oh.

Prue: By the way — congratulations.

Noel: What?

Prue: You won.

Noel: Oh.

Prue *(bursting out):* He's so stupid, I could *kill* him!

Noel: Oh.

Prue: Or I am.

Noel: What?

Prue: Stupid.

Noel: Oh.

Prue: Perhaps I should kill myself.

Noel: Yes. *(Pause)* What?

Prue: Here — are you all right?

> **Noel** *gestures vaguely and goes and sits.*

What's the matter?

Noel: I wish I were dead.

Prue: Well, that makes two of us. *(pause)* I've got some sleeping tablets at the cottage. Shall we go and get them? *(No*

63

smile from **Noel***)* What happened? *(***Noel** *shrugs)* God, you must be feeling *awful* if you can't talk about it.

Noel: If I talk, I shall blub.

Prue: I think I may blub if I don't. Do you mind if I chat?

Noel: Please.

Prue *(pause):* Can't think of anything to say.

Noel *(effort):* Where's Mike?

Prue: He's gone for a walk.

Noel: Oh.

Prue: To get away from me.

Noel *(pause):* Are you very fond of him still?

Prue: It might be one way of putting it, I suppose.

Noel: So am I.

Prue: People have noticed. *(pause)* Would you like me to go away now?

Noel: Oh, no! No! Don't leave me alone — please. *(pause)* Do you think I'm a very wicked man?

Prue: Fairly wicked.

Noel: So do I. I feel absolutely — absolutely —

Prue: You mustn't do that.

Noel: What?

Prue: It's not your *fault* you're wicked.

Noel: No?

Prue: You mustn't take it personally. It's historically inevitable. Like Mike being so thick. Or me persecuting you.

Noel: If only I could believe that.

Pru: Why don't you? It's not only convenient, it's true. *(he smiles)* Ah! A break in the clouds. Listen — I'll tell you something. I was reading one of your books — I like to get to know my enemy, you see.

Noel *(deeply depressed again):* My books!

Prue: Oh, not one of the trashy ones — not the World Atlas of Phallus Worship.

Noel: Oh, *God.*

Prue: A real one. About one of your excavations.

Noel: Oh.

Prue: Before the war.

Noel: Oh.

Prue: It was all one house on top of another. There was this level, then that level, then another level. People had lived on the site for generations. And then suddenly something had gelled, and there was a place which you really felt *had* something. Civilization!

Noel *(bitter):* Civilization!

Prue: Now before, it had just been a place — nowhere very special. And afterwards, it became just a place again, didn't it? Then — generations passed, conquerors came and went, life continued till — Wow! There's this place with *something* again!

Noel: I suppose you could put it like that.

Prue: Well, why be depressed? Same site, different society, new kind of civilization. The process goes on for ever. I like that. I think it's very encouraging. I get a lift just thinking about it.

Noel: Do you?

Prue: Yes. And I'll tell you something else. I think you ought to turn this place into a commune.

Noel: *What?*

Prue: We could sleep twenty or thirty here easily. The tithe barn could be the community centre. We could hold indoctrination classes in the drawing room, and use the dining-room as a crèche. And your study would be just right for holding reviews of individual cases.

Noel: Or torture-chamber.

Prue: What?

Noel: The books would muffle all the cries of pain.

Prue: These flowers will have to go, of course. We'll have to be properly self-supporting. There'll be cabbages in the rose-garden, I'm afraid.

Noel: But you must keep the goldfish pond.

Prue: No. Nothing frivolous.

Noel: For cooling the heels of recalcitrant recruits.

Prue: Listen, I'm talking about a commune, not a prison camp.

Noel: Oh, it may *start* as a commune.

Prue *(pause):* You know what I think? I think pessimism is just a form of bourgeois sentimentality. People can and do change things for the better.

Noel: If it's historically inevitable, I suppose.

Prue: They *do*.

Noel: My poor dear girl, of course they do. Sometimes. But before you reform the future, do examine the past. Everything's been tried. Nothing's worked. It always ends the same way — the prison cell, the concentration camp, the gas chamber, the scaffold —

Prue: Balls.

Noel: In Calvin's Geneva, over half the population went to prison at one time or another. No man was ever made good by persuasion alone. It's always been the whip, the fallanga, the thumb-screws, the electric leads applied to the testicles, the broken bottle shoved up — *(stops himself)* All right. Sorry. I'll shut up now. It's dreadful the way old men tear at the hopes of the young. Birds of prey always go for the eyes. Sorry. Frightful way to behave. I ought to know better. I *do* know better.

Prue: Why do it, then?

Noel: You should know. You think you understand what's best for other people yourself.

Prue: Well, but —

Noel: We're both quite impossible, Prue.

Prue: But you're impossible for all the wrong reasons! You think the world's awful! You think men are beyond redemption!

Noel: Oh, yes — yes.

Prue: *I'm* impossible because I think they *must* be redeemed.

Noel: Ah. You're religious.

Prue: But of course. All true socialists believe man's nature can be changed. Surely you know that much?

Noel: I suppose so. I used to believe it myself, once.

Prue: What made you change?

Noel: Experience. Oh, and self-knowledge. There's nothing like self-knowledge for making you lose faith in the whole human race.

Prue: Look, I see more of the dregs of the human race in court every morning then you've seen in your whole life.

Noel: I doubt that.

Prue: And I have a pretty good idea of what I'm like, too.

Noel: I doubt that even more.

Prue: Only because you doubt everything. You know what?

You're more of an idealist than I am. You're *shocked* by human nature. You're prissy about it. You can't be prissy about human nature, it's self-contradictory.

Noel: But human nature *is* self-contradictory! That's exactly the trouble! And I think any intelligent person *should* be shocked at it!

Prue: And so try to change it.

Noel: But it can't be changed. We're at an impasse, my dear girl. We'll never agree.

Prue: No, but at least we're talking.

Noel (*great contempt*): Talk!

Prue: Don't knock the thing you're good at, man.

Noel: Talk, and talk about talk — that's how my whole life's gone.

> **Jones** *enters.*

Jones: You're up and at it again, then.

Noel: I seem to be.

Jones: Dom Perignon suit you with the sunset?

Noel (*to* **Prue**): Would you like that?

Prue: Yes, please.

Jones: Thought so! Never met a socialist yet who didn't like champers.

Noel: Well, bring it, bring it.

Jones: All right, all right. You go and get dressed. (*Jones exits*).

Noel: Drinking's a terrible mistake. Alcohol's a depressant — people don't realise. They think it cheers them up, but it doesn't. It just encourages gloom and despondency.

> **Francis** *and* **Helen** *enter.*

Prue: And here they come.

Helen: Hello!

Francis: Jones said there was to be Dom Perignon.

Noel: There is.

Francis: Hurrah! I say, Noel, that's a vegetable garden and a half!

Noel: Yes.

Francis: What an asparagus bed!

Noel: Yes.

Francis: I've often thought I'd like to be buried in an asparagus bed.

Helen: Francis.

Frances: Yes?

Helen: Shut up.

Francis: Oh. Right. Sorry.

Helen: Are you feeling all right now, Noel?

Noel: No. But not quite as not all right as I was.

> **Jones** *enters with champagne.*

Jones *(reproachful):* Captain!

Noel: All right, all right. I'll go and change. This dressing-gown is too glum for words, isn't it? I must give it to Oxfam.

Helen: Why not the V and A?

> **Noel** *smiles wanly, and goes.* **Jones** *opens the champagne.*

Francis: Ah!

Jones: Nothing like Dom Perignon on a summer evening.

Helen: You don't think we ought to wait for Sir Noel?

Jones: Lord, no.

Francis: I say, Jones — I mean, is he all right? Really?

Jones: Depends what you mean by all right, Dr Mallock.

Francis: Sometimes he talks as though he was going to pop off at any moment.

Jones: You don't want to take any notice of that. He's always dwelt on death, if you know what I mean. In the war — our war — he was always sure he was going to cop it. When I'd bring him his shaving-water in the mornings, he'd look at me and say, What's the point, Jones? Let the burial party do it, if I've still got a face.

Prue: Ugh.

Jones: Always on about dying, the captain. And then he never got touched. Not so much as a bit of shrapnel, though his mates were buying it left and right.

Francis: Was he — did the men think him a good officer?

Jones: Well, I don't think they paid much attention, really. Officers were two a penny. We were all too busy keeping our heads down to tell them apart.

Helen: Didn't he refuse to obey orders or something?

Jones: Well, he was never much of a one for taking orders, Mrs Mallock. As you may imagine.

Prue: Indeed.

Jones: Handing them out, now — no one better. Ought to have gone straight in as brigade-major, if you ask me.

Prue: But did he actually disobey?

Jones: Lord, yes. Saved a few lives, too. Order came down to lead a patrol into no man's land, just where Jerry'd established a machine-gun. There was some right bloody fools on the staff, I can tell you. Well, Sir Noel said — he was only a lieutenant, then — he said he was buggered if he was going to lead it, and if Captain Meadows wanted it led, he could bloody well lead it himself. So Captain Meadows put him under arrest and told Lieutenant Bartram to lead it, and Lieutenant Bartram, he said the same as Sir Noel, so he went under arrest, too — he was under Sir Noel, and Sir Noel was under him, because there weren't any more officers for them to be under arrest to, if you follow me. And Captain Meadows said, I'll get you bastards if it's the last thing I do, and of course he never did, because he had to go and lead the patrol himself, poor sod. Climbed over the parapet, turned round to call us after him and a sniper got him before he even knew we weren't coming, either.

Helen: My God.

Jones: Buried with full military honours, Captain Meadows was. And Sir Noel, of course, promoted to take his place.

Francis: Typical Noel!

Jones: Oh, yes. He had to write to the widow, and tell her how brave he'd been. Tears pouring down his cheeks. Well — sometimes I thought that war would never end.

Prue: I bet.

Jones: Wine all right, Dr Mallock?

Francis: Wonderful!

Jones *(going):* It's sea-trout tonight. I hope we'll see some better appetites.

Francis: I'm ravenous.

Helen: You always are.

     Jones goes.

Prue: Do you believe all that?

Francis: Oh, I think so.

Prue: I mean it's so unfashionable nowadays to be unheroic, isn't it? All good liberals hold discipline in contempt.

Helen: I certainly wouldn't say *that*.

Prue: I bet a few years ago he'd've been on about how brave everyone was, and stormed machine-gun nests single-handed.

Francis: Well, now you come to mention it — Helen, didn't Jones once tell us something about Noel and a machine-gun nest?

Helen: Of course not.

> **Noel** *enters in a purple velvet jacket.*

Prue: God, you *must* be feeling better.

Noel: Outward appearance only.

Helen: Noel, what *is* that?

Noel: My Grade B American university lecture circuit jacket. It seemed about right for tonight.

Helen: It's not you.

Noel: No. Where's Mike?

Prue: Still walking round Wiltshire.

Noel: Oh. I want his advice. He's so good on the things that really matter. For instance — I'm finalising the plans for my memorial service.

Helen: Noel!

Noel *(producing scroll):* Do you think it would be very ostentatious to have the Archbish of Cant read John Donne's funeral sermon?

Helen: Yes.

Prue: No. Great idea.

Helen: Sorry. Definitely no.

Noel: Right, then I'll have it.

Prue: How long have you been planning this thing?

Noel: Since I was fourteen. I was a very gloomy adolescent. It was all 'In Memoriam' then. Poor old Tennyson — I've eliminated him completely now.

Prue: Let me see that.

Noel: If you insist.

Prue *(reading):* One. Mozart Missa Solemnis.

Noel: I begin with Wolfgang, so I can have him again later on.

Prue: Two. Readings from the Greek Anthology, Horace, Catullus and Petronius.

Francis: In the original?

Noel: In my own translation.

Prue: Three, Verdi's Requiem. Four, Orations.

Noel: That's where the Donne will come.

Prue: Five, Orchestral Interlude.

Noel: Beethoven's Ninth, Mahler's Eighth, a little brassy Berlioz — that sort of thing.

Prue: Six, Readings from the Moderns. Seven, Fauré's Requiem.

Noel: Must have that.

Prue: Eight, Panegyrics. Nine, Lamentations. Ten, Choral Interlude.

Noel: Complete change of pace, you see. A little anthology of English church music. Stanford, Stainer, Samuel Sebastian Wesley, Parry. Even left-wing economists who did well out of Vietnam can be made to blub if you give them choristers in surplices and the high B flat in 'I was glad when they said unto me'.

Prue: Really?

Noel: Oh, yes. I only wish I could be there to see it. Perhaps I can.

Helen: No, Noel.

Noel: Why not?

Helen: I'm not having you starting to believe in life after death at your age.

Noel: Oh, don't be so stupid. I don't mean *that*. I mean, why don't we have this jamboree *before* I die?

Francis: Why not, indeed?

Noel: I'm afraid I might blub. It would never do to be caught blubbing at one's own funeral.

Helen: Noel —

Noel: Yes?

Helen: When's the interval?

Noel: No interval. People might sneak out.

Helen: But they'll have to pee.

Noel: There'll be a font, I expect. There must be a font somewhere in Westminster Abbey.

Francis: The *Abbey*?

Noel: If the Abbey can make room for pretentious American publishers who write flatulent poems and High Anglican verse plays, it can make room for me.

71

Francis: Well, if you put it like that —

Noel: Thank you.

Helen: Won't it be rather expensive?

Noel: Very. But I've decided to blue everything on this one last tremendous party.

Helen: I hope you won't!

Noel: I know you do.

Helen: Not that *we're* expecting anything, of course.

Noel: Aren't you? Really?

Helen: Of course not.

Noel: Oh, thank God! I thought you were. Oh, you do take a weight off my mind. I was afraid you were expecting me to keep my word.

Francis: But you never said —

Helen: Noel —   *Pause*

Noel: You *are* expecting something.

Helen: Not *us*. The college.

Francis: You said a hundred thousand.

Noel: I know.

Francis: You're — you're not —

Noel: Yes.

Francis: But, Noel — the new humanities library — we're going to name it after you.

> **Noel** *shrugs.*

Helen: You said that's how you wanted to be remembered.

Noel: Not any more.

Francis: But look here — let me be candid, Noel —

Noel: Please, please.

Francis: The appeal fund has done very well, considering —

Noel: Well, I did launch it. And the old boys are very sentimental about me.

Francis: But what with inflation and everything — well, the total sounds more than it is. We couldn't even think of starting without your hundred thousand. To tell you the truth, we were going to ask if you couldn't possibly let us have a little more.

Noel: Sorry.

Francis: Look, I realise you feel a little sore about —

Noel: No, no. Well, yes, I did. But not any more. Really.

Helen: It has rather seemed like it. You have rather kept away.

Noel: Yes. Childish. I apologise.

Francis: I was saying to Helen — we can easily do up the Old Brewery for you.

Prue: Very suitable.

Francis: We could make it very nice. There'd be room for Jones, too. *(Prue laughs. Noel smiles)* Don't you want to bring Jones?

Noel: Oh, yes — yes — everywhere. Except Oxford. It's very kind of you, Francis, but I just don't want to go near the place again.

Helen: Noel —

Noel: *No.* No money. No library. Nothing.

Francis: This is a terrible blow.

Noel: I'm sorry.

Francis: What can I say to the governing body?

Noel: Say anything you like.

Francis: They'll want some sort of explanation, Noel.

Noel: Then tell them I've spent my life in humanities libraries, and every second of it wasted. Tell them the groves of Academe have Dutch Elm disease. Tell them my life has been nothing but an example of what a life should not be. That should be clear enough, even for the governing body.

Helen: Noel, you're surely not going to say that all education is pointless just because your own particular work has turned out wrong.

Noel: I'd rather give my money to meths drinkers, to buy themselves a higher class of booze. Let them turn my portrait to the wall. I've done with learning for ever.

Helen *(pause):* When did you write that?

Noel: I didn't write it. It just came.

Helen *(sudden fury):* I suppose it's all going to that boy!

Noel: What boy?

Helen: That Australian!

Prue: Jesus! Is it?

Noel: Of course not.

Helen: To that bogus institute of his at Cambridge, then!

Noel: No.

Helen: Who to, then?

Noel: Whom, Helen — whom.

Helen: God Almighty! You've been rattling that bloody will for twenty years!

Noel: And never changed a word.

Helen: You mean — you mean, you've swanked and strutted over us, and kept us dangling, and — you never meant to do anything for us at all? *(Noel shrugs)* I don't believe it. It's that boy.

Noel: It is not.

Helen: Then it's simple jealousy!

Noel: Of whom?

Helen: Jealousy and spite! Because Francis is a better scholar than you'll ever be!

Noel: *Is* he? *Are* you, Francis?

Francis: I think, Helen —

Noel *(to* **Prue***):* He reads books in French, you know, and calls himself a structuralist.

Helen: You were only ever an amateur! If you hadn't paid for your excavations out of your own pocket, you'd never have got anywhere!

Noel: You're quite right, I'm sure.

Helen: It's always the rich and the dilettanti who get the fame and glory! The people who work, who actually have to *work* — they never get anything.

Prue *(to* **Francis***):* That writes you off, then.

Helen: Francis only got to be master after years of grovelling in *his* shadow! Oh, no, Noel can't resign, no, no — Noel must have an extension — Francis must go on playing Eden to his Churchill! While he ranted and shouted and showed off, we had to wait, and wait, and wait!

Noel: I never thought of myself as Churchill.

Helen: You made our life hell!

Noel: We make our own hells.

Helen: You've treated us as nothing but — servants!

Noel: Oh, no. Never. If you'd had servants —

Helen: *Slaves!*

Noel: Well — I'm sorry.

Helen: *Sorry?*

Noel: I'll tell you what I think. I think we've all been slaves. To a pernicious ideal — the great myth of a liberal education. Teach people to read and write and *think,* and they will become good citizens. Give them history and English and philosophy and politics — teach them to have *opinions.* The more liberal the education, the more opinionated the citizens will be. Raise the school-leaving age! Open new universities! Let there be libraries in every town, and in the country — libraries on wheels! Let the books be free! In a nation of swots and literary critics, there will be no murder, no rape, no thuggery or theft, no grievous bodily or mental harm. Such — drivel. Wicked, sinful, self-indulgent *drivel.* Assuming the best of the human race is in every man. Assuming — How could we have been so stupid? How could we have believed such unremitting cant?

Francis *(pause):* I'm sure you don't really think that, Noel.

Noel: And I am quite sure I do.

Helen: You're just a pathetic self-pitying old man!

Noel: Very probably. I'm sorry if I've darkened your lives. It's partly your own fault for being so servile. But I'm still sorry. My own life hasn't exactly been all sweetness and light. And it's impossible, even in England, to live without casting some shadows. And some people need shadows to thrive in. But — I'm sorry.

Helen: *Pathetic!*

Noel: I'm glad I can still stir some emotion in you.

Helen: You've never been anything else!

Francis: Helen —

Helen: Shut up. You've been asking everyone what you looked like at bad moments, Noel. Well, here's one you may have forgotten. When Francis told you you'd got to go, you looked like a pricked *balloon.* One moment you were all swollen up like a great pink gas-bag, the next you were shrivelled up and *nothing!*

Noel: Well?

Helen: So now you know!

Noel: Yes, indeed. But actually, Helen, I don't care. I've lost interest.

Helen: When your defences are down, there's no one there at all!

75

Noel: Possibly. Or possibly you just couldn't see. You're quite perceptive, but only about things which concern yourself.

Helen: I saw!

Noel: What you wanted to see. So nice you could come. Goodbye.

Francis: What?

Noel: Time to go. End of relationship.

Francis: But you can't just —

Noel: I'm clearing my decks. No more bores. Sorry about the supper. I'll get Fortnum's to send you some caviare.

Francis: Oh, but look here —

Helen: Oh, for Christ's sake, let's go. What's there to stay for? He never gave us anything ever. Thank God we needn't bother with him again.

Noel: That's the spirit.

Helen: I've always loathed and despised you.

Noel: Quite.

Helen: Just as long as you know.

Francis: Now steady, Helen. Noel, look here —

Noel: Run along, Francis. There's a good chap.

Prue: 'Bye.

Francis: We mustn't part like this.

Helen: Don't play into his pathetic hands! Come on!

Francis: Goodbye.

> **Helen** *drags him off.* **Noel** *sighs with relief.*

Noel: That's better. Can begin to breathe again.

Prue: Well, it's certainly *busy* up here at the big house.

Noel: Not quiet.

Prue: Of course, when it's a commune —

Noel: Out of the question. Got a preservation order on it. There's a neolithic camp on that hill there, a long barrow there, two round ones in that wood which no one knows about except me, an iron-age forge behind the barn — very special, that — and I'm almost certain the house itself is built on a roman villa.

Prue: Well? Civilizations have come and gone here for thousands of years. Mine's next.

Noel: Not if I can help it.

Prue: Look, they put a preservation order on King Canute but he still got his feet wet.

    Jones *enters.*

Jones: What the bloody hell have you gone and done now?

Noel: It's all right. We're only one down. This — lady — is staying to dinner instead of the Mallocks.

Prue: Am I?

Noel: Yes.

Jones: I warned you, captain.

Noel: Oh, but they're so *awful,* Jones. I couldn't bear them a moment longer. Dons! Purveyors of learning by the pound — pork sausage merchants!

Jones: Dr Mallock's one of your few friends who actually likes his food.

Noel: No, no. *Your* food. His own is appalling. She can't cook to save her life.

Jones: You're out of hand again, captain. That's your trouble. You don't know what you're like. You don't know what you do to people.

Noel: No. Well — I tell you, if they'd stayed, I'd 've taken to my bed again. And probably never got up.

Jones: Right out of hand.

Noel: Have some champagne.

Jones: I've got some.

    Mike *appears over stile.*

Noel: Ah, Mike, there you are at last. Good. Have some champagne. The Mallocks have gone, thank God. Everyone's gone except us. We can settle down to a cosy family evening.

Prue: A *what?*

Mike: I'm very sorry. I've decided to go back to Cambridge at once.

Noel: Don't be ridiculous. It's midsummer eve.

Mike: I've made up my mind, Noel.

Noel: Out of the question. Jones would never forgive you.

Jones: Dinner in fifteen minutes, Mike.

Mike: I'm sorry. I think it's best if I go straight away.

Noel: Oh, God, now *he* wants a scene. Well, why not? Everyone else has had one. All right, then — but do have a glass of champagne with it. And try to be imaginative, dear boy. Helen was dreadfully predictable — I was so

77

disappointed.

Mike *(careful):* I'm very grateful for everything you've done for me, Noel. But I've decided I'm too old to be anyone's favourite pupil any more — even yours.

Prue: Bravo!

Noel: Quite right. Intolerable position. I sympathise with you whole-heartedly. Now please do sit down. It's so threatening to loom over us like that.

Mike: I'm serious Noel.

Noel: Of course you are. And so am I. Which is all the more reason for being calm, collected and *seated.* (**Mike** *sits*) There. Now we're all on equal terms. Good. Now — first, I apologise to you, and through you to all your predecessors, for having ever put you in such an unenviable position at all.

Mike: Look, I'm not complaining about it, I'm just saying —

Noel: Second, today's whole performance was, really, put on for your benefit. Things began going wrong from the beginning, thanks to your old flame here. *(to* **Prue***)* You were only supposed to be a sub-plot, you know, not hogging the whole day. And then Rupert cut up *much* rougher than I'd planned. He was only *meant* to illustrate the awful sort of Lord Nanny by whom this country's run. So it all ended — is ending as an absolute shambles. But the idea *was,* today, Mike, was to be your graduation day. Pupil was to see teacher as he really was, and the truth was to set him free. As indeed it seems to have done. So we can't say it's all been an absolute failure. Though for me the revelation has been — less than comfortable. A slough, you might say, which I have avoided all my life, only to choke in at the end.

Jones: Now, captain.

Noel: To choke in. The truth is, I did love Harry Somerville. And I never knew it. Couldn't. It went against my principles, you see.

Jones: Harry Somerville?

Noel: Yes.

Jones: I never did like him.

Noel: No.

Jones: Nasty piece of work, I always thought.

Noel: Yes, well — *(to* **Mike***)* You really don't have to go. I know you're angry with me. You have every right. It may be flattering to be fought over at first, but after a time it must be the most awful bore. And undignified. But — End of apprenticeship. I surrender all claims.

Mike: Yes. Well, thanks. I mean, OK.

Noel: Are the cameras ready?

Mike: I'll go and check.

>   **Mike** *goes, glad of the excuse.*

Noel: There. *(to* **Prue***)* Now you and I can be friends.

Prue: Oh, yes?

Noel: Was it all right before?

Prue: Mind your own business.

Jones: That's right. You tell him.

Noel: Make it all right again. If you can. He's very brilliant — quite exceptionally so, they all tell me. And I've seen too many brilliant young men destroyed by jealous young women.

Prue: Jealous!

Noel: Yes. The cleverer the woman is, the more she can't stand the man who's cleverer still. Don't know why. Historically inevitable, I dare say. Don't be like that, will you?

Prue *(pause):* Don't you think you've meddled enough with other people for one life?

Noel: You said I'm not to blame myself.

Prue: Bugger, so I did.

Noel: So now I'm allowed to say whatever I like. However, about that, there's nothing further I want to say.

Prue: Good.

Jones: He's one of the captain's nicest favourite pupils Mike is. I like him. Some of them have been right pricks. That Harry Somerville!

Noel: Ah. Harry.

Prue: You didn't really kill him.

Noel: No. But now I'm wondering if I don't wish I had.

>   **Mike** *appears with a camera which he begins to set up.*

Prue: What's that?

Mike: Just checking the camera.

Noel: Good boy. But don't check it against me, will you? I've been stripped of my illusions today. I'm naked and obscene.

Prue: You still have a few illusions, don't you kid yourself.

Noel: So have you.

Prue: What are you going to do with that, Mike?

Mike: Take pictures.

Noel: It's midsummer morning. We're off to Stonehenge for sunrise. Always go to Stonehenge for midsummer sunrise.

Prue: Really? Isn't it full of Klu Klux men, holding hands and chanting?

Noel: Yes, but we pay no attention. Mike's worked out how much the site has sunk since 2000 BC, and built a little duckhide high above the loony throng to get the sunrise absolutely exact.

Prue: Wow! What if it rains?

Mike: Infra-red.

Noel: And all I ever had to go on was guesswork!

Mike: You can say that again.

Noel: Do you know, I think I'm beginning to feel better.

Prue: It's another illusion. It's only the champagne.

Noel: No, I think it's you.

Prue: Thanks a lot!

Noel: I feel — freer. Not *free,* that would be dreadful, to be completely free. In fact, I think that's what death must be like — complete freedom. But I feel less *burdened.* And look, Jones — there's the evening star.

Jones: Yes, well, I'd lay off that if I were you. You've upset yourself enough for one day.

Noel: Oh, I don't know.

Jones: I do.

Noel: I think these children would like to hear our story.

Jones: Don't, captain. Please.

    Jones exits.

Noel: Once upon a time there was a first world war.

Prue: Oh, good — a fairy story!

Noel: Before *that,* there was a Boer War. My father was in that. He was wounded at Ladysmith. They brought him home on Winston Churchill's mother's hospital ship, and took him to Aldershot. I was only a very small child, but even I could see he wasn't very well. After a year or two, he died. By the time I got to the first world war, no one remembered how it had started or why. We fought because the man next to us seemed to be fighting, and if we didn't, then the man across the way in the enemy's trenches would kill us. Which is exactly why he was fighting, too. And I took one look at it, and thought, This isn't much of an advertisement for western civilization. In fact I thought the Boer War must have been the beginning of the end, and this was the end itself. When a society starts killing off its young men for no particular reason — Well, look at the Athenians, and that disastrous expedition to Sicily. Death wish. Now the obvious thing to do when civilization is committing suicide all around you, is to keep your head down. Don't volunteer, don't speak, don't answer when spoken to. Salute and say nothing. And that worked very well for a time. *(Jones re-enters with more champagne)* Brave and stupid bastards died all round us, but Jones and I were all right, weren't we, Jones?

Jones: Not too bad, captain.

Noel: Give us all another glass. After a time I was Captain Cunliffe, and I began to think I might possibly survive, when some bloody German dropped a shell right on our dug-out. Which promptly collapsed all over us. Bad. Very bad. Worst moment of my life. Buried alive, perfectly conscious, unable to move. Could breathe, though — the timber that pinned us down had trapped some air. But my nose seemed jammed against something soft. His cheek.

Jones: I was just bringing him his water to shave in. Bloody Jerries!

Noel: He couldn't move much, either. Just his head a little.

Jones *(demonstrating):* That much — no more.

Noel: Enough to kiss me. Not done, you know. Officers and men didn't kiss. Absolutely forbidden. Not how western civilization was to be saved. I kissed him back. Nothing sexual about all this, you understand. You don't feel very sexy with several tons of mud on top of your balls. But — to feel another life in that absolute blackness! *(pause)* Everyone thinks I've lived without love. I don't believe anyone, ever, in the whole history of the human race, has felt so much love for another person as I felt for him. When I heard them digging, I hardly wanted them to find us. I knew I'd never be so close

81

to anyone again.

Jones: Only thing'll get closer is the worms that eat you, Captain.

Noel: And I shan't, please God, be conscious of them. It was dusk when they got us out. The first thing I saw was the evening star. Hail to Venus! *(drinks)*

Prue: You've certainly been through it.

Noel: A little. Though for what I don't know. To survive, I suppose. I *did* survive. So did civilization, so did capitalism. The thirties — we were so sure the thirties really were the beginning of the end. And 1939 — that must surely, at last — But no. Now *you* think it's on its last legs, it only needs a violent push, and — But things don't happen like that. They ought to, of course. But they don't. Life isn't based on simple, convenient rules we can all understand.

Mike: It is. Not convenient, perhaps. But probably quite simple.

Noel: Ah, but you mean *physical* life. I mean — social, moral, political, *human* life. What distinguishes us from animals. And there, I sometimes think, there are no rules or principles at all. It's all completely random. There's no *reason* for civilizations to appear. Or too many reasons, which comes to the same thing.

Mike: It does not.

Noel: You can't *create* them, Mike. You may be able to destroy them — little Ms Attila here, she and her friends can blow up everything we call civilization in a matter of minutes, and probably will. But where the next one will come from — God only knows, and he's dead.

Prue: If that's how you really feel, why bother with anything at all?

Noel: Because I'm civilised. I've been taught to bother. Bothering is what it's all been about. I've been programmed to care, so I've cared.

Mike: You don't want to believe everything you hear about brain-washing.

Noel: I don't believe everything I hear about anything. I'm so glad I'm not giving any money to that college, aren't you?

Mike: What?

Noel: I'm not giving any money to the college.

Mike: Why the hell not? It's been your life.

Prue: Who *are* you giving it to?

Noel: No one. I've nothing to give. I gave it all to him years and years ago. *(he means* Jones*)*

Jones: Bloody nonsense, if you ask me.

Noel: I decided I didn't want any ties. I wanted to look at the evening star and feel free. And look what happened.

Prue: Jesus Christ!

Mike: Bloody good, Noel.

Prue: Yes, but — You mean, you worked like a slave for this man all this time, and you had all the money?

Jones: Lot of rot, the whole thing.

Prue: Well, if that's what you feel, give it to me!

Jones: Not bloody likely.

Noel: Never. He's my prop and stay. Everything. All these years we've lived our buried life, and no one's ever known. We've hardly suspected it ourselves. Time has passed, and passed, and there — that has been our life.

Prue: But that's dreadful.

Jones: It's been a bloody good life, thanks.

Noel: It's been a life. Two half-lives, anyway. That must make one life, surely?

Mike: Well —

Noel: Don't tell me, don't tell me.

Mike: If he won't give anything to the college, I think you should, Jones.

Noel: No! They'd only squander it on sociology and history and literature — impure speculation. That's all the humanities are — impure speculation.

Prue: What's so awful about that?

Noel: It's over. Like alchemy. It's served for a couple of thousand years, but now — it's over.

Jones: If you're feeling yourself again, captain, I'll go and dish up. You'll want to eat inside?

Noel: I shall.

Jones: I'll only be five minutes.

Noel: Don't forget the soup.

Jones: Do I ever forget it? Don't either of you two let him pick a bone with you while my back's turned — all right?

Mike: All right.

Prue: O.K., uncle Jones.

Jones: Five minutes.

Noel: All right, all right!

     Jones exits.

Prue: Do we need soup?

Noel: Of course. Dawn can be very cold at Stonehenge.

Prue: Oh.

Noel: Besides, Jones has been making his midsummer soup for years and years. Before the war we used to drive over from Oxford, with half a dozen thermos flasks in the boot. It's fine tonight — shall we walk?

Mike: Isn't it rather a long way?

Noel: You mean, will I make it?

Mike: Yup.

Noel: Don't say 'Yup', dear boy, it's so vulgar. *(Prue giggles)* I suppose you've always been too busy demonstrating up and down it to realise that this path actually goes to Stonehenge.

Prue: Does it? Really?

Noel: Yes. Pity about your ankle — it's a lovely walk. Up a dry valley, and over a ridge with more barrows than you can count — and there's the henge.

Prue: Are you — are you suggesting I might come with you?

Noel: Of course.

Prue: Sorry — I couldn't. Not possibly. We may be friends, but I still have my principles. This footpath should be open to everyone, not just you and your guests.

Noel: My dear girl, don't be so silly! I've given up all that nonsense. Of course the right of way must be kept open.

Prue: *What*?

Noel: In fact, why don't you round up your vandals — tell them all to come.

Prue: Through *here*?

Noel: Yes, yes. It's very bad to fence people out of one's life. Everyone should have a right of way through his garden. It ought to be compulsory. Especially for revolutionaries, like you and me. I hope *you* have one?

Prue: You're *crazy*!

Noel: I'll give the vandals a lecture along the way. I'll tell them why we were all wrong about everything. Are they strong enough to make a litter and carry you? Or shall we put you on a pony? Oh, do come!

Prue *(to* **Mike***):* Shall I?

Mike: Sure.

Prue: O.K.

Noel: Good. It's so instructive, Stonehenge. There it is, there it's sat for all these thousands of years, and we still don't know what the people who built it thought they were doing.

Mike: We do.

Noel: No, no, Mike. We *think* we do.

Mike: It's a sophisticated piece of equipment for predicting the behaviour of the sun and moon.

Noel: Well, we live in a technological age, so naturally we see it as a piece of technology.

Mike: But it is!

Noel: Before us, for centuries, while people believed in God, they saw it as a cathedral.

Mike: Well, they were wrong.

Prue: Couldn't it be both?

Noel: Yes. But not necessarily. It may have been something we can't, in our society, imagine. Just as we can't imagine the future, five hundred years from now. But I bet five hundred years from now people just like us will be laughing at Mike and me for our naïvety and ignorance, as confident as we are that they are right. We never explain mysteries like Stonehenge; but what we say about them explains a great deal about us.

Mike: But we do explain them!

Noel: We get nearer the truth about them, perhaps. The rubbishy speculations of people like me are gradually eliminated. Which is excellent. I rejoice to be eliminated. At least we're not quite as wrong now as we used to be.

Mike: Well — one hypothesis has given way to another more consistent with the facts.

Noel: Exactly. But we never really know. Though it's fascinating what we come up with. I love your computer in stone, Mike. I think it's very elegant. I shall die happy in the knowledge of your hypothesis.

> Jones *enters*.

Jones: Dinner, captain.

Noel: To hypotheses! *(They all drink)* I say, it's been a bit of a day, hasn't it?

Jones: It has, captain.

Noel: But I feel much better than I did this morning: Infinitely better. I feel a great weight lifted. I feel — I was glad when I saw the evening star weren't you?

Jones: Bloody glad.

Noel: Yes.

> He starts off again, then stops.

Prue — give me that thing I wrote to tease those poor Mallocks.

Prue: What thing?

Noel: The memorial service.

Prue: Oh. Here.

Noel: Thanks *(he tears it up)* That's better! On, on! Sea-trout, Chablis, and Stonehenge!

> He leads the way off.

CURTAIN